A Girl from Birkenhead

By Trish Ollman

ISBN: 1539618978
ISBN-13: 978-1539618973

This Book Is dedicated to Ian Ollman, without whom, for the last 50 years, I wouldn't have survived!!!!!

A GIRL FROM BIRKENHEAD

CHAPTER 1

There are many memories that live in the brain of an old girl from Birkenhead. The rumble of the milk man's float as he came up our cobbles and the tinkling of the bottles as he came. Then his whistling as he dropped off the bottles on each doorstep!!! The Rag and Bone man, who came into our street with his horse and cart. There would be a balloon for any kid who donated something to him. Not having gardens, only back yards, the deposits left by his horse were quickly gathered up by my brother who would walk for miles trying to sell it to someone who did have a garden. And the Coalman, always black faced and hands, filthy black clothes and an apron. Heaving the sack of coal into your coalhouse. I know time moves on but haven't we lost such an enormous amount of the good life.

Birkenhead is a seaport opposite Liverpool, on the River Mersey. The recorded history of Birkenhead began with the establishment of Birkenhead Priory and the Mersey Ferry in the 12th Century. During the 19th Century the town expanded greatly, becoming a town as a consequence of the Industrial Revolution, with Birkenhead Park and Hamilton Square being examples of that era. Around the same time, Birkenhead gained the first tramway in Britain. Later the Mersey Railway connected Birkenhead with Liverpool, with the world's first tunnel built beneath a tidal estuary. Birkenhead is perhaps best known for the shipbuilding of Cammell Lairds, and for the town's seaport.

It was 29th July 1952 when I was born Patricia Ann Walsh at Grange Mount Maternity Hospital in Birkenhead. My mother was Hilda May Walsh, nee Davies, and my dad, John Bernard Walsh. They had met a year earlier outside a local picture house and seemed an unlikely pairing. My mum was from a poor working class family, whose father, William Henry Davies had struggled to make ends meet for his family of five on his labourers wage from Cammell Lairds. He'd been in the Merchant Navy as a younger man and in the Home Guard during the War. Her mother, Bertha Davies, nee Osterman, was a lovely gentle lady who kept a spotless house and brought her family up well. However poor though my mother and her siblings were, they were taught manners, how to speak nicely, without the strong Liverpool twang, and to how to keep themselves clean and tidy. My dad, on the other hand, was more upmarket. He had attended St Anselms Private School on a Scholarship and was in line for the priesthood, until his love of women put that to bed for good. He was a good pianist, who could play by ear. He had grown up with a stammer, thought to have been brought about by a fall from a tree when he was seven. His mother, Gertrude Walsh, nee Beresford, had been a servant until marriage. I never knew her, as she died when I was very little. His father, also named John Walsh, had been a Gun Runner in the Irish Civil War and had a price put on his head by the Protestants so had come over to Liverpool to find his fortune and escape. My dad, young John, was the baby of the family and very much idolized. It was with much displeasure when his family found out that he and his lady friend, my mum Hilda, were going to have a baby out of wedlock, so a quick marriage was arranged in May 1952 and I was born in the July. I was to be the first of six children. Next to me came my brother, David, 17 months older, then Peter, who came 16 months later, then Anne, 20 months later, Linda 16 months later and finally Diane who arrived 4 years later. My mum told us that Linda had been born with a rare blood disorder and at 24 hours old had all of her blood replaced. Mum told us how the nurses had made a cross out of wood and covered it with cotton wool when Linda had her blood transfusion. A tall story? Maybe.

I have no memory of my very early years other than my Dad pushing my brother Peter, who is 3 years older than me, in a pram, while me and my other younger brother, David, looked up to a window, standing outside Grange Mount Maternity Hospital, to see my mother waving down at us. She was there to give birth to her fourth child in five years, my sister Anne. My mum threw a Milky Way chocolate bar down at us from her window, which we shared. My next memory is not until I was five. We'd moved to Roker Avenue in Wallasey, Cheshire, into a small but lovely semi detached 3 bedroomed house. Dad worked for the North West Coal Board as a Clerk. I was five and it was my first day at school. Dad had decided he would take me. We stood on the corner of our street and my dad said

"OK. Do you want to go to that horrible school that way (pointing left) or to that lovely school that way (pointing right)?" Naturally I said I wanted to go to that lovely school on the right. It turned out that my Catholic Dad had steered me to start my Education at a Catholic School, and so it was that my first day at school was at St Albans RC School in Wallasey. I've very few memories while there, but one day a tin was passed round our class of five year olds and we were told to put any money we had in it for the poor orphans. (I've always wondered about this as why would five year olds, almost all from poor families, have had any spare money to put in the tin? Nevertheless, I digress!!) When it came to my turn, I pretended to put money into the tin. I've no idea how the teacher knew I hadn't put any money in but she said to me "How much did you put in Pat?" "Sixpence" said my five year old self, who'd never seen sixpence in her life. The teacher took the lid off the tin and tipped the few coins out and there was no sixpence. I was sent to the Headmistress and was given 100 lines "I Must Not Lie"!

The following year my brother, David, joined me at school. My mum would give us a penny each for our bus fares (it was a halfpenny each way) – Again I digress, but who, in this day and age, would let a 5 and a 6 year old walk all the way to the bus stop, over a main road and on the bus to school on their own? We got into the habit of spending the penny on sweets and walking/running to school and home again in the afternoon. One day, David and I decided it would be a good laugh if we went into the church next door to our school and light as many candles as possible before the bell went. In those days, you had to pay to light every single candle. We were happily lighting candles near the altar, laughing away, certainly not paying, when we felt our collars grabbed. It was our Headmistress, a Nun, who, we found out, had been standing watching us. Once again I had to write 100 lines as did our David. I don't know why, but soon after David and I were moved to another Catholic Primary School, St Josephs. At the age of seven, I had pains in my tummy, and, thinking it might be appendicitis, my mum called the ambulance. I can still hear it's clanging bell as it approached our Street. I was ushered onto the bed inside and driven to our local hospital. Once there I was put in a bed in a huge ward. I never did have appendicitis but I stayed in the hospital for a week. Very early in the morning, when it was eerily quiet, all the lights would be turned on and each child would be brought a bowl of warm water, a flannel and a bar of Lifebuoy soap. No toothbrush or toothpaste (that wasn't to come until I was well into my teens and married, but again I digress!!). Once our ablutions were finished the nurse would brush or comb our hair and we had to sit out on the verandah while nurse made our beds. One visiting hour, my dad brought me up a Mars Bar and two Milky Ways, a rare treat. He told me to put them under my pillow, as all sweets were supposed to be handed to the Ward Sister, who would share them all out amongst all the children on the Ward each day. My dad had meant for my sweets to be mine only. Once he'd gone, the Ward Sister, who must have been tipped off, came over to my pillow, put her hand under it and pulled out the contraband. She took it away and I was mortified, especially so when I saw my Mars Bar cut into about six pieces on the sweet plate that came round the ward the next day.

CHAPTER 2

When I was nine, my parents decided to buy a Fish and Chip Shop in Seaforth, Liverpool. On my first visit there, I noticed a small freezer. Inside were two different sorts of ice creams on sticks but they had all melted together. As they were unsellable, us kids were allowed to eat them all. Strawberry and vanilla, all mixed together. What a treat. Running the Chip Shop was hard work for us elder children. We'd come home from school and have to chop and eye the potatoes by hand. We had a metal machine whereby you put the potato in and pulled down a lever and out came chips, falling into a bucket of water below. In winter this was a terrible job because it was so cold you could barely feel your hands and the potatoes were freezing. In the shop itself, there would be a large lump of lard which would go into the fryer. Fish were filleted by my mother and dipped into thick batter and fried until golden. On occasion I was allowed to go into the shop and serve the chips, those times making me feel very grown up. While there, one day, early in the morning, my brother David, for some unknown reason, took my dad's big rusty garden spade out. I was sent out to look for him and tell him to get home at once. When I found him, we were walking back home and David was swinging the spade back and forth. Unfortunately, it went in the back of my heel and severed the Achilles tendons. I fell to the floor and, crying, asked my brother, and another girl who had come over to go and get my mum, who was not far away in the Chip Shop. David came back and said mum had told him to tell me just to "get home now"!! This I couldn't do and eventually she came and carried me the short distance back to the shop. My heal was bleeding, I was crying and our David got the belting of his life. As this was in the school holidays my foot was allowed to heal with a bandage and eventually I was walking on it again, albeit with my foot turned out to the right. When I went back to school, my mum's instructions to my teacher was "if she walks with her foot turned out slap her leg!!" That's how it was for about six months. Then, one day, mum had finally arranged physiotherapy for me and as we waited in the hospital for the physiotherapist, a nurse came in and said that there was a Specialist in the Hospital that day and he'd take a look at me. This he did and as soon as he saw me walk with my foot out he gave his diagnosis that my Achilles Tendons had been severed and I'd need an operation. A week later saw me in the elderly peoples ward (I've no idea why not the children's ward!!) where I had an operation to repair my Achilles Tendons. When I woke from the anesthetic my leg was in plaster from my toes to my hip. I remained like this, firstly in a wheel chair, and then on crutches, for nine months. Incidentally, that operation was to last me just over forty years when I had to have it done again and the Tendons repaired!!! Unfortunately the Chip Shop didn't last. There was another, more established one diagonally opposite us and we were put out of business. My mum told the tale that one night just before we'd closed, The Beatles came in for fish and chips after a gig they'd done nearby. As mum was a teller of tall tales, we'll never know if this was true or not!!!

From the Chip Shop, we moved to another semi-detached house in Crescent Road, Wallasey. We would only be here a year. By now I was eleven and it was time to start High

School. Id taken the 11 plus exam and had got into Grange Mount Secondary School. I can remember the brown and beige uniform, all stiff and scratchy, going on the bus on my first day feeling very grown up. During that first morning in class, I somehow fell off my chair and immediately the teacher said "Oh, so we've got our class clown!!!" Far from it. I was not the happiest or funniest girl a school could wish for. At home, my mum ruled with a rod of iron and beatings were the norm. She would grab me by the hair and pull me down to knee me for even the most minor misdemeanor. Once, she asked me to make her a plate of homemade chips. (Again I digress, but what eleven year old child can be trusted with boiling fat???) The lard was in the dish in the oven, solid. I had to put the oven on until it had melted. This I did, however when I tried to take the dish out of the oven it tilted and the boiling fat spilt all over my foot, scalding me. I, at eleven, was put in my baby sister's pushchair and wheeled by my mum to the hospital half an hours walk away where I was treated for severe burns. I had the scar for years. Back at school, they picked the Class Captain and, as the so called Class Clown, I was nominated. I so desperately wanted this position but it wasn't to be and another girl was chosen, so that lunchtime I made myself the dinner monitor, walking up and down the line of pupils waiting to be served, telling them to be quiet and stand in line!!! All went well until our teacher asked me what I was doing and to get and stand in line myself and be quick about it. My short time as self-appointed Dinner Monitor was over.!!!

Up until I was 11 I spent most weekends and all of the school holidays going to stay with my grandma, Bertha, who still lived in Cardigan Street, just off Conway Street, Birkenhead. The house was a typical brick two up two down terrace in a cobblestone street with a corner shop. Inside, the walls were decorated with the still old fashioned, but popular, brown and green wallpaper and paint and big solid furniture everywhere. The Front Room was for best and I rarely went in there. There was a big tall brown radio but I never heard it play. In the kitchen, the stone sink did its work, with dishes, and us, getting washed in it. Every week, just the once mind you, we would have a strip wash and wash our hair. Out the back, there was a concrete yard with a homemade woodshed and the outside toilet and coal shed. I use to tie a piece of rope to the door handle of the toilet door and the other end to the back door, put a cushion on the middle and use it as a swing. I fell off it backwards many times but it never put me off. Then there was playing two balls up against the wall: One potato, two potato, three potato, four. Grandma was a lovely kind and gentle lady with white hair, even though only in her early 60s. Because she had a heart problem, she slept downstairs in a metal single bed with a big fluffy eiderdown on it. I would sleep with her, next to the wall. At home, I was the eldest of 6 children, brought up in an unhappy home, with no nurturing, playtime or books. So to go to Grandmas was for me a lovely treat as she spoilt me with love and kindness, something I never got at home. In the school holidays, when I was staying with my grandparents, Monday to Friday, at 5.30 am on the dot Granddad would come downstairs and put the kettle on then light the fire. He used small pieces of wood that he could get from Cammell Lairds, twisted bits of yesterday's Daily Mirror, then once it had caught hold a few pieces of coal would go on. For some reason he never turned the living room light on, only the kitchen light and the flames from the fire would dance round the room, making patterns on the ceiling. Granddad would then bring us a cup of tea. I can't remember him ever having breakfast, then with his flat cap on he'd brave the dark on his bike to ride to Lairds. I would lay in bed with Grandma and watch the patterns of the fire on the ceiling. It was magical. Grandma and I would get up around 9am and get dressed. Sometimes we did the washing in the big copper tub, then use the big mangle to get the water out of the washing, other times we would go into next door to her sister, my Auntie Annie, and have a cuppa and a chat, then sometimes we would go to Grange Road to do our shopping. Blackledges and Sayers were my favourite shops. There, you could get deep filled blackcurrant tarts, strawberry and cream tarts and, my favourite, cream filled meringues. I would split the two halves open, eat the fresh cream, then the two halves of meringues one by one. Walking back home with our groceries, Grandma, with her bad heart, would have to stop and sit on a wall to catch her breath. Then, on the dot of 12.10pm Granddad would come home, carrying his 2 bundles of wood from work and every day eat the same lunch, Heinz Scotch Broth with a piece of bread. His Daily Mirror at his side he would pick out his gee gees (older readers will know these as race horses) and head back to work. Grandma and I would then put our coats on and take his bets down a back alley off Conway Street and put on a Yanky Bet, or his tanner each way. (Betting off the track was banned back then!!) I don't think he ever won much but he enjoyed his ritual as much as he enjoyed his mundane repetitious life.

CHAPTER 3

My life changed when I was 11. One early morning, I was awakened by my brother David telling me that Grandma had died. I went downstairs and saw my mother crying but making us porridge to eat for breakfast before going to my Granddad. We went on the bus and I can remember thinking "why are all these people smiling. My Grandma just died". We were ushered into the living room one by one where my Grandma lay dead in her bed. I noticed she had no pillow and that half her face was a dark blue. My Mother made me kiss her on the cheek and I was repulsed by it. All of my brothers and sisters were crying but I couldn't shed a tear. I'd been Grandmas favourite, the one shed spent the most time with, yet I couldn't cry for her. We were all ushered outside into the back yard when the Funeral Directors came for her. I never really said goodbye and us kids weren't allowed to go to her funeral at Landigan Cemetery. She'd died of pneumonia and pleurisy.

Afterwards, I continued to go to Granddad's house but it was never really the same. I'd just go to Grange Road and do a bit of shopping for him. I'd lie in bed listening on my tiny transistor radio to Radio Luxemburg. He wasn't an affectionate man and we had no real bond. He carried on working at Camell Lairds but died almost a year to the day after Grandma of lung disease. While they were still alive, every year, from when I was seven until I was eleven, my Grandma, Granddad and Auntie Annie, Grandma's sister who lived next door, went on many a Hardings Coaches Day Trip. They were the highlight of my childhood. We'd go on 3 or 4 separate day trips in the summer holidays. Llandudno, Rhyl, Southport and Blackpool. There was always a new dress and knitted cardigan for me, I can remember a brown one and a green one, and new white ankle socks and sandals. We'd meet Aunty Annie in the back entry, then there was the short walk up Parkfield Avenue to the little sweet shop on the corner. A quarter of our chosen sweets for the journey then on to the coach at the top of Claughton Road. There was a real sense of excitement and camaraderie as we drove under the Mersey Tunnel (a HUGE treat) then onwards to our destination. The Mersey Tunnel had been built to connect Birkenhead with Liverpool and it was a magical place. There was a Tollbooth at the entrance where the coach driver would have to pay the fee, then into the darkness, with the smell of diesel and the rats running alongside the road. The journey through the tunnel only took about five minutes but it was like another world to me. Once out on the other side, in Liverpool, we would head out towards our destination, if it were Blackpool or Southport. If it was Blackpool, there would be many false sightings of the tower but they were only electricity pylons!! Once there the Coach would park in a designated parking area for coaches. We would then stop at a Café and have a 3 Course Lunch at 5/- a head. Greedy me would have 2 deserts!!! What a treat it was. Granddad had saved Pennies all year for me to put in the One Armed Bandits, or we would have a tram or horse and carriage ride along the Prom. Then there was the Fairground. Rides on the Caterpillar and the Walzers sent my head spinning but Oh what fun. The noise, the colours, the people. After the fair, Granddad Grandma and Auntie Annie would all find a Pub and sit me on the wall outside with a bottle of pop and a bag of Smiths Crisps, the ones with the little blue bag of salt in them, while they went inside for a Pint and a Port and Lemon. All too soon it was time to go home, back onto the Coach, then the drive down The Mile to see Blackpool's famous Light Display. Our trusty Hardings coach would take us home with everybody joining in a singsong. As we returned back through the Mersey Tunnel, a cap would be passed round for the driver. We'd stop at Claughton Road and make the short walk home. All too soon the day had ended and we fell into bed exhausted.

After Grandma and Granddad died, all eight of my family moved into their two up two down terraced house in Cardigan Street. We never had any treats or pocket money, all the things today's kids get. By now, my parents had had a sixth child Diane, having had Linda a few years earlier. So going over to our big city of Liverpool was the height of adventure!! We only went once a year, at Christmas to the Grotto. We would alternate each year, doing Lewis's Grotto one year then Blacklers Grotto the next. How fabulously exciting was it at Lewis's to go in one door, into a dark Room with twinkling stars on the ceiling, sitting in a big wooden sleigh, then a mysterious voice telling us that the sleigh would be taking us to Santa's grotto. Christmas music would start and the sleigh would rock back and forward. Then, lights would come on and we had to exit by another door into that most magic of places: Santa's Grotto, complete with 2 female Elf Helpers and a gift for all. I must have been 13 or 14 before I realised the magic of it all and we really hadn't travelled anywhere at all!!! We were so innocent and naive. Then there was Blacklers Grotto with their Dancing Waters, spouts of water fountains all lit in different colours, all dancing to music. Then into the Grotto where, on the wall, there were hung 2 groups of presents: GIRLS on one side, BOYS on the other. Pencil cases, plastic dolls, toy guns, whip and top, skipping ropes, all laid out for us kids to make our choice!! Oh how excited we were. And how grateful for such a magical treat!!! And how hard it must have been for our poor parents who could never make ends meet on Dad's Cammell Lairds wages, to pay the half-crown each for us 6 kids to get a present off Santa in the Grotto!! Happy days indeed, and the one day of the year Mum and Dad were truly proper parents!!

CHAPTER 4

Back in Cardigan Street, every Saturday we'd get up and have our cornflakes or toast. No fancy sugar-laden cereals then. My brother used to have toast with dripping and salt on!!! Sundays were Salt Fish breakfast or Kippers with that exotic BROWN BREAD and best butter. Back to Saturday, more often than not, while my Grandparents were still alive, I was to be found at Grandma's house. After breakfast, while Granddad put more wood on the fire, it was time to clean the brasses with Brasso. That smell!! I loved it. Then Id be tasked with brushing the floor. No Vacuums then. Dishes to wash, bed to make. Then the time was my own. We never went anywhere. The weekend shopping had mostly been done the day before and what other things we needed were bought from our Corner Shop, run by a lovely little Irish woman called Rita. Here, in this shop, not only could you buy basic groceries but also, to my childish eyes, lots of lovely sweets. Barley Sugar

Twists, Sherbet Lemons, Sweet Tobacco, Little sweet cigarettes with a red tip in a box, making you think you were very adult while holding one between two fingers and pretending to smoke. Pear Drops, Black Jacks, Walkers Toffees, Fruit Salad, Milk Chews, four for a penny. Galaxy and Caramac Bars where my favourite, as well as Treacle Toffee. I could only buy sweets legally when I was at Grandmas as mum and dad never gave us money for any when I was at home. On the weekends that I was home with the family, my brother and me would have to take the weeks washing to the Launderette on Conway Street. We would take it all in our Diane's pram, in blue plastic bags. As there was 8 of us there used to be quite lot of washing to do. We used to get three sixpences for the clothes dryer but we would spend one of them on MILK CHEWS or BLACK JACKS. Mum would always wonder why the clothes weren't properly dry when we got home and would have to hang them on the overhead pulley above our dining table. Then it was paste butties for lunch washed down with watered-down pop (there were six of us children and my mum and dad, and dad would pour him and mum a small glass each then fill the remainder in the bottle up with water and divide it amongst the six of us kids!!) We then all had to go out for the day to Birkenhead Park, where we were instructed not to go home till it was dark!!! Being the eldest I had to look after the younger girls. We'd run up and down the hills and go on the swings for hours and look at the ducks on the Lake, innocent pastimes and we were safe. No harm ever came to us and no bad men ever took us away. Sunday was Sunday School and JESUS LOVES THE LITTLE CHILDREN!!! How I hated Sundays. There was hardly anybody about and little traffic on the roads. Reading and singing about Jesus was never my thing, even though I was being brought up a Catholic. After Sunday School we would go home for a roast dinner, something I am grateful to my mum for doing, then back to the Park to finish our weekend off. Oh and don't forget Songs of Praise and The Black and White Minstrels Show on the Tele!!! Then back to school the next day.

Twice in my childhood, my dad announced that we would all go to New Brighton Baths for the day. Oh what heaven. That blue water and hundreds of skimpily clad men and women, the splashing sounds mixed with the smell of candy floss and chips, the massive diving board. The fountain seemed huge but seeing pictures of it now it looks tiny. I was to go again when I was about 14 with my brother, who had joined St John's Ambulance. We went for the full day and attended, along with a Leader, to minor cuts and injuries. One man came in suffering from heat stroke. David and I felt very grown up as we held a flannel to his head and gave him sips of water. The best bit about the day for me was that we'd got in without having to pay and we got to swim for a while in the afternoon. The St John's Ambulance Leader had bought a load of sandwiches with him, which he shared with us. I vowed then to also join St John's Ambulance but I never did. New Brighton was very close to Birkenhead where we lived. Not only did it have a fabulous Open Air Pool but an indoor and outdoor Fairground. In its Victorian heyday, thousands would descend on its beaches and enjoy dipping their toes in the sea and the pleasures the town had to offer. Ice creams and Donkey Rides must have seemed like heaven from the usual every day drudge. We went there once a year with my parents, on Whit Sunday. Being six children, we were only allowed to choose one ride each. My brothers and me would usually chose a stall where you won a Prize Every Time!!! There were no Ice Creams or Candy Floss for us but Mum would take paste sandwiches and the watered down bottles of pop and we'd sit on the beach happy as Larry till it was time to get the bus home. Somehow, we knew there was very little money and we just accepted our lot. We never felt sorry for ourselves or wished for more.

The beginning of each November saw myself and my two brothers excitedly building our Guy for Bonfire Night. Once we were happy with the head, which was an old sack stuffed with newspaper, then an old jersey and a pair of pants for the body, we'd sit it in our Diane's pushchair and push it around the streets, knocking on doors, and going into the pubs before the Landlord could order us out. For some obscure reason, my mum would always expect us to give her the money we'd collected, but before we did, we would buy ourselves some sweets before handing over the rest of the cash to her. When the big night itself arrived, we would all go to our Uncle Billy's house in Leasowe and join our cousins for the bonfire and fireworks party. Uncle Billy, my Mums brother, had three children and worked for most of his life at Cadburys in Moreton. He used to be allowed to bring home the seconds, my memory always remembers a chocolate bar called Bar Six which he brought home the most. Once we'd eaten a supper of toasted crumpets, our Guy would be ceremoniously pushed to the bonfire, which had been built by the local children on the corner of their street, and once it was well alight, we would throw it on. The air was magical. Sharp and so bitterly cold you could see the steam coming out of your mouth as you talked. The fire would be crackling away and the occasional piece of burning wood would be spewed out. There was a party atmosphere as friends and neighbours huddled together in groups. Soon the fireworks would be let off. Bangers scaring the elderly, rip raps chasing people down the street. Catherine Wheels spinning. Dogs barking. Remember how all the fireworks had great sounding names. Blue Flame, Golden Showers, Rainbow Stars. We were never ones to put fireworks through people's letterboxes but we knew of boys who did. We'd wait until the fire was nearly out, running around playing tick or some other game then it was back to Uncle Billy's for hot chocolate, something we never had at home, so a rare treat. Bonfire Night was one of the highlights of our year. Magic!!!

CHAPTER 5

There was a charity called Thompsons Mission at the end of our street. My brothers and I would go on Thursday evenings for a obligatory religious service, which didn't bother us, as we got to sing JESUS LOVES THE LITTLE CHILDREN at the top of our voices. But it was all worth it because at the end of the service you lined up and got that holy of holy's, A FRUIT BUN!!!! Some kids used to throw theirs at each other (they were somewhat stale!!) but we devoured ours as if they were milk and honey. Being so poor, it was a weekly treat!! Then, back there again on a Sunday where, after the obligatory religious Service, we got to choose one of the dozens of items on the stage. These were all secondhand but could have been a toy, some shoes or an item of clothing. I once spied a pair of scuffed white sling back shoes with a tiny heel. I was about 13-14 and coveted them more than I had ever coveted anything before. At the end of the Service I pushed my way to the front of the queue, eyes glued to the prize. Finally, Oh Glory Be, the shoes were mine. In the corner, off came my dirty white galoshes and, with whitish ankle socks, the new Holy Grail of shoes were put on. They fitted and I was truly in heaven. I tottered back on the cobbles of our entry in my tiny heels, and in to show my mum. Instead of singing my new shoes' praises she belted me round the head and screamed at me to get them off AND TAKE THEM BACK RIGHT NOW!!! I was mortified. Hearing her shouting at me that I looked like a tramp (and I don't think she meant the homeless kind!!!) I made my way back to Thompsons, shoes in hand. Unfortunately by the time I got back almost everything from the stage had gone. I was left with the choice of a jigsaw of a train or a vacuum flask!!! I chose the flask!!!

After my grandparent's death, our family of 8 took over the lease of their two up two down house in Cardigan Street, just off Conway Street. There was also a tiny box room, which we made into another bedroom. My life there, at the age of 12 to 16 was not a happy one. Mum and Dad were always fighting, there were never any nice, encouraging words spoken to any of the six of us kids. No sports or extra-curricular activities. No talk of our future careers or education, things my own grandchildren take for granted now. My only pleasure was going to Birkenhead Library and taking out an Agatha Christie book. I'd read all of them by the time I was thirteen and ready to start all over again. I went to school in a motley collection of clothes, never the proper uniform the only girl in the school without one. One time one of my shoes broke in school. I walked home in the dinner break without shoes on and was given 6 pence by my mum to go to Exmouth Street and find another pair. The shop in Exmouth Street was a dark and dank place run by a woman whose elderly mother, dressed all in black, sat in an old fashioned big chair in the back room. You could see her from the shop. On three sides of the shop were long trestle tables piled high with single shoes of all shapes and sizes. After finding one that might be suitable (and don't forget it was the age of The Beatles and I was 13-15 at the time and wanted to be modern) the search would then begin for its twin. Many a time saw me run out of time before having to return to school and taking the only pair of shoes, often boys ones, that we could find two of and that fit me.

When I was twelve, my sister Diane was born. She was named after the Frank Ifield song, My Diane. I'd come home from school one day to find my mum sitting by the fire knitting, an unusual sight in itself, then her telling me I would be having a little brother or sister. I can't remember being excited. Life in our house was pretty grim so I suppose I just thought the new baby was just another one for me to look after. One day, some months later, we five children and my dad walked my heavily pregnant mum to the bus stop, where she was to catch a bus to the Hospital to have the baby. Dad was to stay behind at home to look after the rest of us. I remember Mum saying she wanted to light a cigarette but if she did the bus would come. Sure enough, that's what happened. I still have a vision in my head of my pregnant mum getting on the bus with her little brown suitcase and us five kids and dad walking back home without her. The next time I saw her she was carrying a small bundle of baby, wrapped in a pink blanket.

And so the sixth and final Walsh baby was born. Our Diane. Being twelve, I had to look after her a lot. Change nappies, feed her, try to stop her from crying. One day when she was around one, I had to take Diane in her push chair to the newly opened supermarket on Conway Street for some groceries. I got home and unpacked the few bits then sat down with our David to play a card game. After a good half an hour, mum, who'd been next door talking to my Aunty Annie, came in and said to me in a panicked voice, "Where's the baby?" I experienced one of the worst panic attacks I've ever had. I'd left her in her push chair outside the supermarket. I've never ran so fast in my life, fully expecting her to be gone. But no, there she was, asleep in her push chair as though nothing had happened. Needless to say I was never allowed to forget that for many months to come!!! It was from that same supermarket that my brothers and me would steal sweets. My sweet of choice was a box of Maltesers. I would casually walk round the small supermarket then grab the Maltesers and put them under my arm. I was never caught and this gave me the impetuous to go and steal again and again. As the supermarket was only a short distance away, it took some feat to try and eat a whole box before getting home. But this I did, albeit with great difficulty, in the back entry of our house. Maltesers are not the easiest chocolates to eat, especially when shoved by the half dozen into ones mouth.

I would gobble them up as quickly as possible but had to suffer the residue around my teeth for ages afterwards. One of my brothers was the master chocolate thief. From the same supermarket, he would wear a long coat with quite a few inside pockets (obviously a thief's coat!!) and inside these pockets he would stash Galaxies, Mars Bars, Cadburys chocolates, Curly Whirlies, you name it he got it. Down his socks, under his arms. Anywhere he could hide something. There was obviously no Store Detectives in them days. At lease we had sweets, something we'd never really had, apart from our Christmas Selection Box, until the opening of our first supermarket. I hasten to add that I've never stole anything since I've become an adult!! But back then, stealing was usually, for us kids, the only way of our getting sweets.

CHAPTER 6

When we moved back to the house in Cardigan Street in Birkenhead after Granddad had died, I was enrolled at Conway Street School, a short walk from home. Unfortunately my mum never felt it necessary to buy me a school uniform and I was the only girl in the school without one. My sisters would suffer the same fate, although the two boys, who went to The Birkenhead Institute, had a full uniform each. One day, I was visiting my Aunty Edna, who, with her husband Uncle Michael, ran The Charing Cross Hotel. I was allowed to wash glasses in a sink next to the till and saw a Tip Jar which had a number of half crowns in it. I'm ashamed to say that I took two of these half-crowns when nobody was looking and put them in my pocket. I'd seen in Woolworths in Grange Road a pleated skirt (our school uniform skirt was straight) and a light blue (whereas our uniform was navy blue). They also had white blouses. A perfect choice on which to spend my ill gotten gains, I thought. At least Id have some semblance of a school uniform. I made a quick trip into Woolworths and the items were bought. How to get them past my harridan mum though. That was a problem. But I found a solution. And so it was that every single school day morning I would get changed in our back entry and hide my non uniform clothes and change into my new ones. There was a large standing stone near the bottom of the entry and I'd hide the clothes behind that. I'd do the reverse after school. Even though I still stood out at school I felt better. It wasn't to be for my poor hair though. It was the age of The Beatles and Rock and Roll and straight hair with a fringe was what every kid my age wanted. I have naturally very straight hair but here was no way my mum would allow me to have a fringe. In fact I couldn't even have it straight. She had a curly perm and so thought that my hair must look like hers. She made me put in metal curlers and pipe cleaners every nigh and each morning I had to brush my hair out until I looked like a golliwog. I despised it and would often stand in our back entry crying, spitting on my hands trying to straighten my hair. What a sight I must have looked every day at school with my ridicules hair and non uniform. One day mum decided I should wear a new pair of socks that shed bought me. Now bear in mind that every other girl in the school wore white ankle socks, these new socks where made from red and white diamonds and were knee high length. As I had no other socks behind my secret stone in the entry I had no option but to go to school in them. When I walked into the playground, everybody in sight looked at me and started laughing. I had to wear those socks for many months until I somehow found a way to steal another sixpence to buy myself an illicit white pair.

My five siblings and I were divided into two groups, Me and my two very close in age brothers, and the younger three girls. The three youngest didn't even enter our radar. My brothers and me went everywhere together causing what mayhem we could. Our David would always play the funny man. He would hide behind hedges and jump out at old ladies, causing almost fatal heart attacks, but somehow we thought it funny. He would take a bottle of milk from somebody's doorstep, take the top off and drink half of it, before putting the silver top back on and replacing it. Even better if it was a bottle of the orange juice the milkman used to bring. Another time he would go up to a random stranger, with me and Peter hiding a few meters away, and ask if they had sixpence for his bus fare home as he had no dad and his mother had twelve children to feed. Very often he would come away with the spoils. Night times were often hard on us three bigger kids. As the girls slept in one bedroom and the two boys in the other bedroom we would often shout along the corridor to each other when we were supposed to have been going to sleep. Many a time, all of a sudden, we would hear "Come down you three". We knew what we were in for. For just talking, we would be lined up and hit on the hand by my dad with whatever happened to be the implement of the day. Be it dads belt, a metal coat hanger, even the bread knife. For most of my life I have felt the injustice of this, as my dad was actually quite good to us the rest of the time and I don't know why the odd shout across the small corridor upstairs bothered him and my mum downstairs. Our Peter was the thief of the house and we would experience the same treatment if mum found something missing. In her bag she kept some sugared almonds, the only sweets, apart from our Christmas Selection Boxes that were ever in the house. She knew to the exact one how many sugared almonds she had in her bag but sometimes Peter would take one and we'd all be called downstairs for our punishment.

As there were six children in our household, we were entitled to free school dinners. Every Monday, my teacher would read out a list of children who were booked to have dinners. Then at the end she would then say "And Pat Walsh, you can have free school dinners". This used to mortify me, as I was always ever the only one to get dinners free. Free or not, boy did I enjoy them. The Hall was always transformed by the Dinner Ladies into a wonderful canteen with long tables and chairs. We sat in our class areas and went up to the serving tables where such delights as mince and mash potato or mince with a pastry crust on top, cabbage or peas and gravy were served by the ladies in their white coats and hats. I'm sure we must have had mince of some kind every day as neither myself or my husband can ever remember having anything else. Pudding was always either Spotted Dick, blancmange, or Jam Roly Poly. On each table would have been put a metal jug of custard. By the time we got round to it, a lovely thick skin had formed and luckily for me nobody else on my table would entertain eating it, so I got the skin every day. Even in the school holidays we were able to get school dinners, albeit from a different school. I suppose it was the Governments way of making sure us poor kids had a decent meal, even when school wasn't on. Sunday Tea, however poor we were, was usually always special. We would have the left over roast meat from our Sunday Roast – Mum couldn't afford a decent joint so would go down to the Market around 5pm on the Saturday and pick up a Scrag End of lamb cheaply. She would roast this, with carrot and turnip, roast potatoes and Oxo gravy. Yummy. Nothing like it ever!! – after the meat buttties we would often have Trifle: Jelly (always red), jam roll in it, or maybe a tine of pineapples or peaches if there was the money, and false cream on top. I would be sent mid Sunday afternoon to Hursts Bakery on the corner of Claughton Road and Parkfield Avenue, to get a bowl full of the false cream for a shilling. Naturally, being a little piggy, I would use my finger to scoop up the cream and into the mouth on the way home, so when I arrived, there would only be half a bowlful. Mum used to complain that Hursts were getting stingier by the week with their cream.!!! With most of the people in Birkenhead being lower class or "poor", Sunday was the one day of the week when a mother could really try to put on a good spread for her family. A roast dinner was usually the norm on a Sunday lunchtime and there was always a special treat for most at tea time. There was a boxed Trifle, Birds, that tasted nothing like what mum made but was a welcome treat. And for those who were in the money, a tin of salmon, put onto butties. Battenberg cakes, Eccles Cakes, Jam Tarts, Apple Pie or just homemade Jam Sponges, all were welcome treats from the mundane weekday food. In summer, the Ice Cream Man would come and some mothers would take a bowl out and get the man to fill it up with the lovely soft ice cream to go with whatever they had planned for Sunday Tea. We had a tiny food safe in our small kitchen. There was nothing edible in it, only flour, salt, sugar etc. It was a wooden box cupboard with a metal mesh front. My brother David found a way of lifting the metal mesh up at the corner when my parents were out and gaining access to the inside. As there was nothing in it we could readily eat, we would make 'toffee' out of sugar and water. It was the most horrible thing ever but to us, who had nothing else for an evening snack, we thought it was OK. One of our favourites was Mums Bread Pudding, which she made occasionally. Nothing remotely like today's version, Mum would soak stale bread in water overnight and squeeze out the water the next morning. She would then add the other ingredients (if only I could ask her now what they were!!) and steam in a metal bowl with a lid with a little red handle on top. When it was done, hours later, the pudding would be solid and firm, and turned out of the tin. It would then be left to go cool and sliced. Never tasted anything as good as it.

CHAPTER 7

When I was 13, I was given a record player by my aunty. It was only a second hand one but it opened a whole new world for me. Amazingly, mum let me take it into the front parlour, that holy of holy's that nobody ever got to go into, and it was here that I was to hear my first record, The Beach Boys Sloop John B. I'd persuaded mum to let me buy The Jackie once a week and had posters of The Beach Boys on my wall above the bed. I soon learnt how to change a needle on my record player's arm and listened to that record over and over again until one day my dad got so fed up with hearing it he gave me enough money to go out and buy my second record, a Cliff Richard one. No idea now what it was called but he was my number two favourite heartthrob. In the mid 60's you either liked Cliff Richard or Adam Faith, Liverpool or Everton and were either Catholic or Protestant, and you hung round with a like minded group of friends. With my budding record collection I now had the start of what would, within three years, become 'My Collection of Singles'. We still went over to Liverpool once a year, just before Christmas, and told to chose a toy that we would like. When I was 13, in Lewises, I chose what was to be my last doll, as I had recently discovered that I wanted to be a Hairdresser when I left school. This was only a smallish doll but she had lovely long blond (nylon) hair and came with a tiny plastic hairbrush. Once we'd all chosen our toy, it would be off to the top floor Café for 3 egg and chips between us 6 children, while dad had a pie and mum had a toasted teacake. She used to take a packet of 'best butter' with her in her handbag and would slyly add more butter to her teacake from her stash. I suppose my dad would have gone back over to Liverpool at some stage to buy the chosen toys as they were always on the bottom of our beds on Christmas morning. Isn't it funny, even the worst childhoods have some happy memories and mine are no different? Christmas Eve in our house was magical, even when I was in my early teens. We would have tea, then all sit down and write a Christmas card for various aunties and uncles then watch a festive TV program then up to bed, where we would hang one of our socks on the end. Being

December, the air would be bitter in our unheated house (save for a small coal fire in the living room), sometimes our breath coming out as we spoke. We never really had blankets just old coats on our beds. No sheets or pillowcases. We'd never even heard of such things. I'd lay in the darkness, no longer believing in Father Christmas, but waiting for my dad to come up with the presents. The anticipation of it was better than the actual event itself. Then, I'd hear him come quietly up the stairs. My two sisters were long asleep and Id close my eyes but squint ever so slightly so that I could just about make dad out. There would be a rustle of paper and a weight near my feet while dad laid us girls' presents out in three piles. I have to say, how mum and dad did it I do not know. We always had a good Christmas. (The following year I asked for a typewriter as I then wanted to be a writer and I got one; an old black Underwood with the black and red ribbon. I found out years later that dad had put it under his coat in his office at Cammell Lairds and walked out with it!!!). On this particular year, there was my doll with her long blonde hair along with, probably, six other small presents and, as was usual at that time for us, a box of chocolate liquors from Birkenhead Market. The chocolates themselves were in the shape of a bottle, with a chocolate shell, a coating of sugar inside and a funny tasting liquid in the center. They were all labeled 'Crème de Menthe', 'Gin', and 'Scotch Whisky'. We thought we were so grown up. I realised many years later there wasn't a smidgen of alcohol in them. Once dad had gone back down the stairs, I would sit up and try and feel through the wrapping paper what presents Id got. This was excitement personified and I was able to fall asleep happy. We always woke early, as do todays kids, on the big day and amongst much shouting and wrapping paper, our presents were revealed. Us three bigger kids always ate all of our liquor bottles straight away, while still in bed. Then we'd take our spoils downstairs to play. My new doll's hair was brushed and put into every conceivable fashion, with clips to hold it all in place. We never wanted breakfast as we'd eaten our chocolates but Christmas Dinner, again another feat of glory for my poverty stricken parents, was a masterpiece. In those days, Chicken was only for the rich but mum would do a leg of lamb with mint sauce, roast potatoes and cabbage, with thick Oxo gravy, then Christmas pudding with custard. And we all got a cracker with a paper hat and useless plastic gift inside. The afternoon was spent playing with our new gifts until the

Christmas movie would come on our tiny Redifusion TV set. All eight of us would find somewhere to sit, mum having pole position on the couch, sharing with our Peter who would promise to tickle her feet if he could have the other seat, and dad on the easy chair with the rest of us kids on the dining chairs. Tea would be a simple affair of a boiled egg and soldiers and maybe a Trifle, then into next door to see my Aunty Annie who, amazingly, would give us three bigger children, who were still only in our early teens, a tiny bit of sherry in cut crystal glasses. All too soon Christmas was over and we had the long week to wait for New Years Eve to come. We spent our time going to Birkenhead Park, even though it was freezing mid winter, and just generally hanging around making nuisances of ourselves. New Years Eve was much anticipated by us three older kids as we got to stay up. It was a long and boring evening, watching Jimmy Stewart on the TV, singing his old fashioned Scottish songs and the Highland Dancing but at a minute to the magical hour, dad would put on his hat and coat, pick up his piece of coal and head out of the back door to meet up with all the other men from our terraced row of houses. The countdown was on the TV and soon there would be a sharp knock on our front door as dad, wanting in from the cold, welcomed in the New Year. The fog made the ships horns on the Mersey eerie but amidst us all singing Auld Lang Syne, a happy time was had by all.

CHAPTER 8

In the New Year, when I was 14, I went looking for a Saturday job. I found one at a Hairdresser in Exmouth Street, washing hair and brushing he floor. I worked from 9am to 5.pm and for this I was paid two shillings and sixpence, all of which I had to give my mum. This job for me wasn't without its hazards as on a number of occasions I would burn the heads of what seemed to me to be little old ladies who'd come in for a shampoo and set with water that was too hot. I felt very grown up now, having a real job of my own. However, one day my mum came into the salon and got talking with the owner. She persuaded her to give me a tight perm, something, which I deplored. And so, one Saturday afternoon when we weren't busy, I was given a tight curly perm. I was mortified by my new appearance and when I got home could not stop crying and looking at myself in our tiny mirror above the sink. Mum must have had enough of me as I got a good belting and told to shut up and get up to bed without any tea. I've always felt that mum resented me and wanted me to look ridicules because I was grandma's favourite and the only one of us six children that grandma would take on days out each year. Whatever the reason, she was particularly cruel to me.

One year, after we'd moved into Cardigan Street (I would have been about 14) we all piled into my dads new car (I cant remember the make but it was tiny) and after meeting up with Uncle Billy and his family (My mum's brother) we made our first journey as a family out of Merseyside. We drove all the way down to Somerset and Devon, complete with roof rack and full camping gear that mum had got from the catalogue on tick. The six children were all somehow fitted into the back, with the younger ones on the older ones knees (no seatbelts in those days!!), some bottles of water and a pack of paste butties and dads trusty AA Map, which mum had opened out on her knee. We left very early in the morning so by tea time we'd reached Somerset. A suitable camping ground was found and the tent, with some difficulty, was erected by my dad and two brothers. It was a very big tent with an annex and an awning and we had a Calor Gas stove and a big plastic bucket for water and all the other necessities. You could hire bikes to cycle round the local area but such extravagances were not for us. I would have loved to do that but it wasn't to be. However, all of us kids would go down to the stream and play quite happily there for a few hours. Then it was time to go into the next field and collect a bucket of apples off the trees there. Now, believe it or not, at 14, I had never even seen an apple, never mind tasted one. The apples we picked were cider apples and very bitter and it was to put me off apples for the rest of my life. My brother David, though, ate them like sweets. We woke up the next morning to two things that will stick in my mind forever. The smell of fresh grass after a lifetime living in concrete and bricks was like nectar to my nose. I only have to smell freshly cut grass nowadays to be transported back to that morning. The other thing that sticks in my mind is the mooing of the cows. Id never heard them before. I got up and went out of the tent and the grass was wet underfoot, my first experience of dew. I think I could have lived there forever but soon enough dad and the boys took down the tent and we moved onto Devon. On our way down to Somerset from Birkenhead, our Diane, the youngest, had been grouchy and whingy. On the morning we packed up for Devon, a large lump had appeared in her neck, so the first thing we did when we arrived in Devon was to find the nearest hospital where poor Diane had the large lump removed in A & E and stitches put in her neck. We took it in turns to have her on our knees in the back of the car for the rest of the journey, even though my other two sisters, Anne and Linda were only small themselves and took it in turns to sit on my brothers' knees. We soon found a camping site from our AA Book of Caravan and Camping and once again set up the tent, this time it would be for a week. While there wasn't much money for petrol, we did manage to drive over the magnificent Dartmoor National Park, with its ponies wondering round at will. I remember Dad stopping the car and us all getting out as a group of about six ponies were eating the grass. Five of them ran away but one, a brown and white one, stayed and allowed us all to touch our very first horse. The landscape of Dartmoor was something we'd never seen before and was made all the more magical because of it. Grassland for as far as the eye could see, its one of those places where one could build a little cottage and live happily ever after. Another treat was the picture postcard village of Cockington. With its very old buildings and thatched roofs, archetypical country church, and manor house, it was one of those places you never forget. It was here that we had our first ever afternoon tea of scones with jam and clotted cream. Mum bought 4 serves between eight of us but being served a cup of tea in a bone china cup and saucer was the highlight of the day. We had a trip into Torquay with its many fish and chip shops and gulls hovering overhead while we tried to eat our chips. There were bars of striped rock and big babies sweet dummies. Boxes of fudge and treacle toffee, all with 'A Present from Torquay' written on the front and a picture of the town center. All too soon our first ever holiday was over, the tent packed up and piled on the roof rack then back home, mum with her trusty AA Map on her knee and the six of us all jostling for space in the back of the car.

Amazingly, the following year, a month before I was 15, we again went camping, but this time over on the Ferry to France, Switzerland, Belgium and Luxemburg. Where my parents got the money from I will never know, even though we would travel third class. As a sulky almost 15

year old, Europe held no interest for me. I bitterly resented
having to look after the younger children and was always
last to be served lunch or dinner because I was the eldest.
Amazingly, even though we were camping, we still had a
pan of homemade chips, done in two lots, every night for
tea, over the Calor Gas cooker. I can remember going into
a small corner shop in Calais and trying to buy bread and
milk. I came away with it eventually, but without a single
word of French it was hard going. My only other memory
is of being in Switzerland and seeing all the shops lit up
with their windows full of watches and of having terrible
toothache there, which my mum fixed by soaking a bit of
rag, which she always kept in her bag, with TCP, her cure
for all ailments under the sun. On our last night in Europe,
we found a camping spot in the dark and set up the tent.
We were awakened the next morning by a policeman. We'd
set up on the grassy knoll of the beach!! On the way home,
driving through London, all six of us packed into the back,
one of my brothers said I'd elbowed him. Mum turned
round from her front seat and started hitting me and
digging her nails into my arm, nothing have had enough
because he pulled over, somewhere in the unusual in that.
My dad, who was much kinder, must of had enough of it

and told her to stop. We were in the Centre of London, and he told mum he'd had enough of her hitting me. She stormed out of the car followed by my brother, trying to get her to get back in the car. I'm not sure what happened next but I got out and started to walk in the opposite way to which my dad was parked and my mum had walked. And I kept walking. To this day I do not know why my dad, who was still in the car, didn't stop me. I was still only 14, a month away from being 15 and I was walking away. After a good half hour walk I reached a main street and got on the first bus that came along. It was to take me to Battersea in South London. In those days, if you didn't have your bus fare you could give your name and address to the conductor and pay at a later date. As I had no money at all, this is what I did. I got off the bus at a long row of shops, with no plan in my mind. As I walked, I passed a Tobacconist shop and in the window was a card with the words "Nanny Wanted for 3 children" and then the name and address of the advertiser. There was an old cigarette box on the floor and I had a lipstick in my bag and wrote down the address off the card. I went into the Tobacconists and asked for directions to the address. When I arrived there, there was nobody home. It was in a large block of flats, so I sat and waited on the stairs. After about an hour a man appeared. His name was Tony and I told him Id come about the job. I think at that time I probably looked older than my years as he never questioned my age. I told him I was 18 and had lost all my luggage on my way down from Liverpool. He told me he had three children, aged 6,8 and 13 years. I was given the job on the spot and he later took me out to his local pub to show me off. I later found out he was 37 so to bag an almost 15 year old must have been his prize. I met the children and they were very welcoming. My job was to get them out to school in the morning, do the housework and shopping during the day and make dinner in the evening, bath the two youngest and just generally look after everything. I also had to be a wife to Tony, and even though I was only 15 I took on this role only to keep my new job and for somewhere to live. For weeks afterwards, every noise outside I would think was the Police come for me. Tony would give me ten shillings a day for housekeeping but I also had to buy myself some essentials out of this money as I had nothing, so I visited various second hand shops there. I felt so grown up and domesticated that I even painted the bathroom one day a hideous blue. Tony told me that although he didn't like it he could live with it. Before I'd ran away, I'd met a boy called Ian 'Olly' Ollman back in Birkenhead, and one day, Tony gave me enough money to go back up to Birkenhead on the train to see him. Id written to Olly at his parents pub, The Angel Inn in Beckwith Street, Birkenhead, from London and, even though we'd only known each other a few months, I put at the end "I still love you". Ian, which was his real name, wrote back to me and also finished his letter with "I still love you too". Hence Tony paying for me to go back up and see him. We managed an evening together while his parents were in the pub – remember I was a run a way – and I left him at 11pm just before his mum came up from the pub. Unfortunately I had nowhere to sleep and no money to get back down to London I decided the churchyard at St Werburghs Church at the top of Grange Road would offer me a place to sleep but when I lay down on the grass in the corner a tramp came and sat next to me. I ran for dear life and decided to hitch hike through the Mersey Tunnel over to Liverpool. I made my way to Lime Street Station and sat all night on a bench there. Ironically, a policeman came over to me and asked what I was doing there at 2am in the morning, and I told him I was waiting for the 6am train to London and he left me alone. Amazing as I was a WANTED runaway!! Once it got light, I again hitch hiked back through the tunnel to Birkenhead and started the long journey hitch hiking back down to London. I arrived back at Tony's place quite late, let myself in and found him in bed with a blonde. I slept in with one of the girls that night and the next morning packed my things and walked out. I went to the nearest railway station, having not a penny to my name, and found a copy of the previous night's newspaper laying on a bench. I looked in the Situations Vacant column and there was a job, again for a live in nanny. It was in Hendon, North London. I went to a phone box and reversed the charges to the number given. I was given the address and asked to come that afternoon for an interview. But how to get from Battersea in South London to Hendon in the North? I did the only thing I could do and that was to catch buses, giving my name and (false) address to the conductors. I remember nothing of the interview, but I was offered the job and asked if I could start straight away. No references were asked for or given (amazing to me now) and I started that night by feeding the two small girls that I was to care for. I was given a small room with a single bed , a wardrobe, chest of drawers and a chair in it. The following morning, the mother said she'd teach me how to cook the meals they liked. Being Jewish, they didn't have my usual of deep fried chips and egg but dishes using lots of butter and cream. It was here that I would first start to put on some of the weight that would follow me right throughout my life. I was only at that job for maybe a month. I never felt comfortable around the family plus I had been writing to Ian and our budding relationship was growing. One day, I just packed my bags and left. Once again, having no money, I hitch hiked back up the M1 to Birkenhead and headed for Ian's pub. He was babysitting his sister's four girls that night. They lived in a house adjacent to the pub, and as we sat on the couch, the girls all in bed asleep, Ian said to me that he needed to go next door to the pub and get a packet of cigarettes (He'd been smoking from a very young age due to the accessibility of cigarettes in the Pub). I noticed that he'd been gone a long time then suddenly I heard footsteps coming up the stairs to the living room. A sharp knock on the door and then the biggest Policeman I'd ever saw came in. "Pat Walsh? You've caused us a lot of trouble young lady. We've been looking for you." My stomach plummeted to the floor and I felt sick. I'd been away for four months; I'd dyed my hair and had a mini skirt on and a face full of make up. I was escorted downstairs by the Policeman to see a sheepish looking Ian standing at the door and my mother!!! The look on her face when she saw me (keep in mind the curly perm and red knee high socks!!) made me feel even sicker. There were THREE Police Cars out the front of the pub, which was a bit of overkill for a fifteen year old run a way I thought, and all the drinkers from the Pub had come outside to see what was going on. I was led, shame faced, into one of the police cars with my Mum. We were taken down to a Police Station near Woodside and I was asked questions as to where I'd been, who I'd been with etc. When I was allowed to go, after being read the riot act, Mum and me got the bus back home. My dad was out but my brothers and sisters were all home. When they saw me they all gasped. Purple hair, black eyes and red lipstick, plus a mini skirt and wedge heeled shoes. It didn't help matters that I took out a packet of cigarettes and offered my mum one!! She told me to put them away and that we'd have to wait for my dad to come home. It was a nervous hour before we heard the front door open and dad walked in. He took one look at me and said, "Get in the front room". Once in there he told me that he wanted me gone the next morning, as I was a bad influence on the other five kids. I was ordered to get in the kitchen and "take that rubbish off your face". Looking back now, I can imagine their horror. Just before I went up to bed, my usually mean and nasty mum said to me "Do you want to stay home?" When I answered her "Yes" she said she'd have a word with my dad and that was it. It was never mentioned again. I found out that when Ian had gone to get his cigarettes from the Pub, he's previously been instructed by both his and my mum to let them know the next time I was in Birkenhead and where I was. Ian had told his mum that I was next door at his sister's house and so the Police were called. I didn't see or speak to Ian for the next two weeks but we got back together soon after. I was actually grateful to him as I'd got sick of London and of being a run-a-way and just wanted to be home again.

CHAPTER 9

I'd met Ian in the usual way. I had been 14 when I was allowed out to go to the Boys Club with two friends, Linda and Joan. The first time we went there we went up to the indoor gallery and looked down to see a five-a-side footy match being played. Joan who knew most of the boys pointed to the goalkeeper in the red polo neck jumper and said "That's Olly". We then went to the kitchen area to make a cuppa and shortly after the boys joined us. In those days you mostly carried round any records you'd managed to get in a plastic bag and as there was a record player in the Club wed put on some songs and have a dance. We did this for a few weeks and one night, one of the other boys said to 'Olly' "why don't you carry Pat's records home (I was, and still am, Pat to my family?") The Procol Harem Song was playing, 'A Whiter Shade of Pale' and someone commented on the fact that 'Olly's' skin was so pale that night. He did indeed walk me to the end of our street. And we stood in the doorway of the corner shop. I found out that his real name was Ian Ollman, hence the 'Olly'. We said our goodbyes and I realized he hadn't even tried to give me a kiss as all the other boys Id been out with had. Soon I was going round to the pub his parents ran, The Angel Inn in Beckwith Street. They lived above it on one of the three floors; the upper floors being closed down and almost derelict. Ian and I would play our records on his record player, plugged into the light socket and sometime babysit his sisters 4 girls who lived next door. I had left school the previous July but Ian had stayed on to do his 6th form CSE's so was still at school. It was a slow courtship but things took their course. It wasn't until Ian and I had been going out together for about almost a year that he went to Spain for a week with school that I realized how much I missed him. I even went round to The Angel and made an excuse that Id left my jacket upstairs just so I could go in his bedroom and smell his jumper. Ian and I spent longer and longer together, in fact every opportunity we could. I was very unhappy at home and glad to get out and see him. His brothers and sister were very much older than him and had families of their own, leaving Ian to amuse himself every day while his parents ran the Pub. We would stay above the Pub playing records, Ian's arm slowly going around my shoulders. It took a long time for the first kiss. Ian was extremely shy but one day it happened and I'm not sure who, out of the two of us, was more shocked, me or him!! When I came back from London, I had applied for, and got, a job at E. R. Squibb and Sons who were Pharmaceutical Manufacturers in Leasowe, opposite Cadbury's. My job was as Office Junior. I had to do all the odd jobs, photocopy on the old Gestetner Ink Copier, make the girls in the Typing Pool their cup of tea, deliver the mail, all easy stuff. But I was made for greater things, or so I thought, and soon had the girls making their own tea and getting people from other departments to come and get their own mail. In the Typing Pool we had a big Tele Text Machine. It was like a giant typewriter with a phone attached and you telephoned into whoever you wanted your message to go to then typed your message. On my second day there, I was shown this machine and explained how it worked, so in the lunch break, when all the other girls were in the canteen, I decided that I would give it a go and send my dad a message on it. Now Dad worked in the highly secret Polaris Submarine Planning Office at Cammell Lairds. I looked in the Directory and found

Cammell Lairds phone number, dialed it, got the tone and started to type. What I didn't realize was I had the Shift Key on and instead of writing "Attention John Walsh. Polaris Planning Office. Hi Dad. How are you? I am doing well at work. See you at Tea time" I'd actually wrote ##@***(%$$### (you get the drift). Now, as this was live, this message was what Cammell Lairds Tele Text Machine received. I hung up and decided to try again the next day. Around two hours later I was called to the Managing Directors office, where two plain clothes policemen were waiting for me. I had caused an almighty security breach at Cammell Lairds with my message and my poor dad had had to subjected to hours of questioning about any relationship he had with any foreign people who might have sent him that message. It was soon sorted out when they realised what I had done but my dad gave me an almighty tongue lashing when I got home that evening. He'd nearly lost his job over it!! While at Squibbs, I can remember having a mini dress and one day our Supervisor in the Typing Pool asked me to stay behind after the other girls had gone home. She told me that in the canteen where the entire factory workers had their lunch, whenever I leaned over to get my tray at the counter, you could see my knickers. Now today, that would not be that big a deal, but in 1968 it was unthinkable. I couldn't wear that dress again.

I started going ice skating after work, on my own, to the Silver Blades Ice Rink in Prescott Road in Liverpool. Being short of money (or having none as was usual in my case) I would hitch hike through the Mersey tunnel and do the long walk to the Ice Rink in Prescott Road. I loved it. Not long after I started going there I could speed skate and loved whizzing round and round on the ice. I also had a few lessons and had mum make me a costume out of Gold and Red lame material from Birkenhead Market. I asked some of the girls from work to come with me and once or twice a few did but mostly I was on my own. One night, the DJ asked me to have a drink with him. We went across the road to the pub and I had my usual Vodka and Lime (I was still only 15!!!). The DJ 's name was Bob Wooller and he told me he'd been the DJ at The Cavern and had given The Beatles their first gig there. I've read many books on The Beatles and Bob Wooller's name is always there. Not long after, I decided that being an Office Junior was not for me and I soon found work as a typist, even though I couldn't type, at British Rail Headquarters in Liverpool. Within my first hour there, they realised I couldn't type (I didn't even know how to turn the electric typewriter on!!) and transferred me to the Drawing Office as a Junior Clerk. Every day while I was there, I would get back on the train at Liverpool Central and get off at Hamilton Square and meet Ian. I can't remember us ever having any lunch, just a kiss and a cuddle on one of the benches in the Square's garden, then back on the train to work. Every Friday after work, we would go into the Capitol Chinese Restaurant near Hamilton Square and have Curried King Prawns and Rice. I'd pay as Ian was still at school but it was our weekly treat. Each evening I would go home, get changed, grab my bag of records and go round to Ian's. It was a relief getting out of our two up two down house and my five brothers and sisters as well as my cranky mum. By now, we did more than kiss and, with his parents down in the pub every night we were free to do as we pleased. And we did.

CHAPTER 10

All was going well until one April day I went to the Doctors because I was feeling sick all the time. After some tests, and to my shock, I was told I was pregnant. I was still only 15. Ian was just 16. In those days you got a Milk Book sent to you by post if you were pregnant and that's how my mother found out. My milk book came in the post. Having been what I now think of as a rotten mother, she suddenly became a rock. She asked me if I wanted an abortion (NO) and if I would like her to go and see Ian's mum. I said yes to this as his mum was such a harridan and I was terrified of her. My mum tried on quite a few occasions to get Ian's mum to give her consent for us to get married but she wouldn't. (Looking back now if it was my 16 year old I wouldn't give permission either!!!), however we were determined to get married and keep the baby. Back then, in England, you had to be 18 to get married without parental permission). We found out that you can marry without consent at age 16 in Scotland so, in late July 1968, and without Ian's parents knowing, We set off from Hamilton Square Station, with 6 pounds in our pocket, to start the long journey to Gretna Green (by Ribble Bus!!) from Liverpool. But when we arrived at Gretna Green there was a huge new Police Station, which immediately scared us as Ian was a 'run away ' so we stayed on the bus and got off at it's destination of Edinburgh. At the bus depot there was a B&B which we wearily booked into, spending 2 of our 6 pounds. The following day we were looking for somewhere to stay and came across a Rental Agency on Princess Street where we got a attic room for $2.50 a week. After we d paid for this we had a pound left which didn't last us long. The following day we found a pawn shop and pawned Ian's new electric razor, his camera and the second hand gold ring Id brought with me to get married with. We put up the bans in the Morningside District Registry Office the day I turned 16 a few days later. We had to wait 7 days before we could get married. Not many memories from that time other than, at 4 months pregnant, I got my first horrible morning sickness, and the fact that we ran out of money again and had to get my dad to telegram a 10 shilling Postal Order to us. The big day arrived, 6th August 1968. Id washed my bone coloured coat the night before and it was still wet. Ian had impetigo on his face so I stuck bits of plasters all over them. What a sight we must have been as we turned up to Morningside Registry Office. First thing the Registrar asked was "Where are your Witnesses??". We hadn't a clue we needed any, so we went out into the street where we got little old ladies to come and be our witnesses. As I had no wedding ring, one of the ladies lent me hers to get married with. After a brief ceremony we were man and wife. We had no money to pay the fee!! Then one of the ladies who had acted as witness gave us a pound note. Finally we were able to pay the ten and six for the Licence. After the ceremony, we went next door and had a cup of tea with the change from the pound note then went back to our digs and collected our bag. We got the Ribble Bus back home to Birkenhead with no tickets. When the Inspector got on (there was no conductor) I showed him our one-way ticket that we'd used to get to Edinburgh and told him that we had bought the tickets in Birkenhead. I doubled the price we'd paid for the tickets and the Inspector said the clerk in the booking office must have made a mistake. And so we got home without paying!! We also got home to face the music from Ian's mum, who was horrified when I told her we were married. She gave us "6 months"!!! (She even tried to get the marriage annulled!!) 48 years later we re still together. What an adventure for two young kids!!

After we got married we tried living with my mum and dad for a few day but it was obvious it wasn't going to work out. There was no room for us anyway as there were still 5 other children at home, and my mum was still being mean to me. So, against my better judgment, and without a choice, we moved into The Angel with Ian's mum and dad, Chris and Ted Ollman. Living at The Angel was no better than being at my mums. Naturally, Ian's mum resented me for getting pregnant and for marrying her youngest son when he was only just sixteen. Because she was always downstairs in the Pub, I never saw that much of her, thank heavens. Ian had got an apprenticeships with Spillers Flour Mills on the Docks and was earning five pounds a week. I was able to buy a maternity dress, which I wore every day of my pregnancy, but money was short. Ian, a smoker, would often have to buy a 'Penny Loose' Woodbine and have to walk to work (a fair way away) as he didn't have the bus fare. I'd got my first morning sickness when we'd eloped to Edinburgh and I had it until the day I had Stephen. Every day was the same. I tool pills to help but they never completely stopped the vomiting. Years later I was to find out that other women like me, with morning sickness, would be given a drug called Thalidomide, which would leave thousands of babies born with horrendous deformities. I was lucky. My pregnancy flew by. I got very big and had terrible back pain and as Christmas 1968 approached I longed for the birth. Not having much money, we bought a cheap cot and a secondhand beautiful big Silver Cross pram. Nobody helped us out with anything. My mum and dad didn't have much money and they still had 5 children at home, but Ian's mum and dad only had themselves to look after but they never once helped us out with anything. A few days before Christmas, it was bitterly cold. I had my appointment with the doctor to see how everything was going, as I was only a week away from giving birth. I begged the doctor to admit me and start labour off as I was at the end of my tether with the pregnancy, as most mothers are at that stage. He agreed and I went into Grange Mount Maternity Home in Birkenhead. It was three days before Christmas. On the first day they tried giving me castor oil to bring on labour.

That never worked but gave me shocking stomach cramps. The second day the Doctor broke my waters, and later that afternoon, my labour started. I remember the pains being very intense right from the beginning. I was in a labour ward with two beds, but on my own. Nurses were coming in all evening saying it was snowing outside and later that night one of the nurses fell down the stairs and broke her arm. Just before my labour began they'd given me some spotted dick and custard. That soon left my stomach as labour progressed!!. By the middle of the night my pain was one long continuous one and I was so high on gas and air that whenever the nurse came to see me I could see four of her!!! Come Christmas morning, the nurses knew I wanted a girl so they wrapped the cot my baby would be put into with pink tinsel and baubles. At 6.40am on Christmas Day 1968 my first son, Stephen Kenneth, was born. He didn't breath at first and the nurses worked on him for a short while but luckily he was OK. He weighed 6lb 14oz. Ian and I were sixteen. The nurses hastily changed the colours of the tinsel on the cot to blue and so we became parents of a baby born on Christmas Day. During Christmas dinner, back on the ward, the hospital doctor came round with his wife and two children and gave me a gift of a little bowl, plate and knife and fork set for Stephen. Ian was allowed to come up to Christmas dinner and brought me gifts from home. It was a beautiful time. The following day, the local newspaper, The Birkenhead News, came round and took a picture of Stephen and I and in that week's addition, there was a picture of me with a baby Stephen with the caption 'Only Boy Born On Christmas Day". I still have the cutting.

CHAPTER 11

I was sent home from hospital after seven days, as was the norm then, and began life as a Mum. I got no help from anyone, as my mum lived on the Woodchurch Estate, a fair way away, and Ian's mum was in the pub working and socializing all day and evening. But I somehow managed. I think I was a lot more mature than the sixteen year olds of today and I had mostly brought up my five brothers and sisters. My periods, when they started again, became irregular, and after a while I went to my doctor. He put me in hospital for a Curette (where they scrape the womb out). I was in my hospital bed, shaved, pre med given and in my gown, when the doctor came in, pulled the curtains around my bed and told me that my urine sample had told him I was pregnant again. Stephen was only around 10 weeks old and I was not yet seventeen. I think the worst part was going back home and telling Ian's mum!! Naturally, we got on with it and life went on. As I grew bigger with the second baby, looking after Stephen became harder. Ian's mum would get Ian in the living room on his own when he came home from work and tell him that I'd stayed in bed all morning and that I hadn't washed the nappies. I hated her. I also hated that Ian never once stuck up for me, but he was only a boy himself!! On 5th January 1970, a year after giving birth to Stephen, our second son, Martin Ian John was born, again after a long induced labour, at St Catherine's Hospital in Tranmere. He weighed 7lbs 11oz. I had already had my big Silver Cross Pram made into a twin pram, by adding another hood onto the other side, and a new twin storm cover made, so we were pretty soon out to the shops in Grange Road and back to normal. Life in The Angel was horrible. I still got no help with the two babies and Ian's mum still resented me. His Dad. Ted, was much kinder and he and I, while the babies slept, would often have a quiet half hour while the Pub was closed for the afternoon, having a cuppa and a cake whilst having a chat. Desperately we searched for a place of our own. Someone told us of a flat off Conway Street. It was in the basement of a house lived in by a very old lady. It was in a terrible state but, excitedly, we took it on and started to go round after Ian got home from work each night and do it up. We ashamedly stole money from the pub till and bought those horrible foam ceiling tiles and put them up. We painted and cleaned for weeks. But it was awful. You could hear the old lady's TV so loud it shook the room. The stove was so filthy with grease, it wouldn't come off, however hard we tried. We decided we didn't want to live there and 'sold' it (We'd furnished it as well) to a girl who lived over the road from The Angel for fifteen pounds. She gave us five pounds deposit and we gave her the key. We never saw the other ten pounds. So life at The Angel went on. Eventually we heard of a house in Peel Street which was up for rent. It was old and run down but we jumped at it. We moved in with hardly any furniture but after two weeks there we decided we couldn't stay there either as it was too run down. So we went back to the Angel. We'd applied to be housed by the Council and a short while later a lady came round and told us we'd been allocated a two bedroom Flat on the new Noctorum Estate. We were ecstatic. The following day, after all the paperwork was done, we got the keys. The flat was brand new, and had never been lived in. it was the most beautifulest thing we'd ever seen. I remember being completely impressed with the round sink in the kitchen. I'd never seen a round one before. We moved in with our motley collection of furniture, donated by various family members and my life truly felt complete. I would stand looking at the various rooms every evening when the boys had gone to bed and just stare in wonderment that this was all ours. A week after we moved in we got a letter from the Council telling us we had to move out as they had received 'information' that we'd lived in the Peel Street house and hadn't declared it to them. We were devastated. We tried to fight it but it was no use. They wouldn't listen. Through a Residents Group on the Noctorum Estate we heard of a Church which had a house in Tranmere that had just been finished being done up by volunteers. We contacted the Church and, after many interviews and talks, we were given this house to rent. It was in Holbourn Hill, Tranmere. We were moved in there within days and it became our home for the next 3 years.

During these three years I tried my best to bring the boys up well. I dressed them in matching clothes and always made sure they had everything they needed, even though we were poor. Ian had moved on to a job at Cammell Lairds. Every payday, me and the boys would meet him out side work and walk to a café in Charing Cross and have egg and chips. This was an expensive meal as it used to eat into what was left of his wages for the week. Many a time I'd have to hide behind the couch when they came for the rent!!! One Christmas Eve, I left the boys with Ian and went down to Birkenhead Market to do a few last bits of Christmas shopping. When I was trying to pay for my first purchase, I found my purse had gone. In panic, I went to the Police Station but it hadn't been handed in. The Policeman directed me to the Citizens Advice Bureau, which at the time was in Hamilton Square. The lady there must have felt really sorry for me, with two small boys at home, and on Christmas Eve. She produced a tin with 'Emergency Fund' on the front and in it was a five pound note, a full weeks wages for us. She gave me that five pound note and I went back to the market and bought what I needed. I also stopped off at the small Tesco's Store on Grange Road and bought my first ever turkey and some other groceries and got a taxi, again a first, home. Imagine my disbelief when I got home to find Id left my purse on the table. I'm ashamed to say I never gave the fiver back to the Citizens Advice Bureau, but it was one of the best Christmases we had!!! By the time Ian and I were 19, we had the 2 small boys and were living in Holbourn Hill off Old Chester Road. He had been out of work for 6 months when the government told him he had to take a job anywhere in England. The only one he was offered was as a pallet maker in Herne Bay KENT!! Hundreds of miles away. We never really got on with either Ian's or my family, so it was easy to make the move. Plus he had no option but to take the job, and on 5th January he packed his bags and left for Kent. I was left behind with the two boys, eagerly awaiting him to contact me with the news that he had found us a house to rent. I waited for him to send me a telegram (no phone in those days) saying that he had found us a house, but nothing. He said that there was only one Estate Agency in Herne Bay and they had nothing at all to rent, not even a room. Being ever the impatient, action not words person I am, on 10th January 1973, a week after Ian had left, I packed up our little two bedroom house, got the Government to come and take our furniture into storage and said goodbye to Birkenhead, again this seemed to me to be an easy thing to do. I met Ian at the train Station in Herne Bay. We had 7 pounds between us (which we thought a fortune) and we got a taxi to a hotel on the seafront. That took up most of our money so once again we were broke, but this time we had nowhere to live. The following morning, a Saturday, Ian had to work till 12. As we had to be out of our hotel room by 10am, I left the luggage behind the hotels reception desk and made my way in the freezing cold, one boy in the pushchair the other holding on, to the only Estate Agents in town, sure that Ian hadn't been pushy enough when he'd gone in. But no, he'd been right. They had nothing at all to rent. All of the Boarding Houses were full of off season students so not even a room. I walked back up the promenade to the hotel pushing the pushchair, crying my eyes out. By this time it was snowing and we were frozen. We got back to the Hotel and waited for Ian to get back from work. The manager was very nice and said he had a friend who had a MENS BOARDING HOUSE at the top end of the Prom. He gave him a ring and was told there was a vacant room; but that a man was due to take it in 7 days time. We could have it though till then. When we got there we found it to be a tiny room on the top floor with a single bed and a one burner oven cooker. We were charged $3 for the week. The Hotel had been $3 for the night, so we had a pound left. The owner was very good and brought us up a folding camp bed for the boys. With the pound I bought a tin of

Fray Bentos Pie, a tin of potatoes and a tin of peas. I'll never forget that meal. I was just so relieved we had a room, at least for 6 nights. For the next few days we walked around Herne Bay trying to see if there were any empty houses, then one day, oh luck of luck, we found an empty mid terrace. I went to the council to find out about renting it but was told that it had been condemned 8 years ago, was uninhabitable, and couldn't be lived in. On our last night at the Boarding House Ian and I lay in bed trying to work out what to do. We decided to break into the condemned house and see if we could some how make it livable. We had no idea of the extent of its condition and in our young ignorance thought we could 'Do it Up'!!! The following morning, after packing our belongings, we went round to the house. We'd envisaged Ian having to break in somehow but would you believe it, the front window opened easily, first try!! The boys and me waited on the corner, convinced Ian would have to break a window to get in, but no, it was that easy. Once we got inside it was plain to see why the house had been condemned. There was 8 years worth of junk mail which had been pushed through the letter box so it was hard to open the door but we got in happy as Larry!!! Ok so it had big bits of roof missing, holes in the stairs and no electricity, gas or water. Not even the toilet in the back yard worked. But for now it was ours, albeit illegally. While Ian moved the 8 years worth of junk mail from the hallway, I went to the phone box and rang to get our furniture delivered. (It was in London. In those days, if you were relocated by the Government for work they stored your furniture free of charge until you found somewhere.) Ian went and bought candles and a new door lock. When the furniture van arrived at 4pm it was snowing and frozen. The driver looked at the house and said YOU CANT STAY HERE!!! But I had to tell him that's all there was. He was very upset but unloaded our things into the downstairs front room. It soon became apparent that we were going to struggle without the bare necessities, such as water, power and a toilet. By this time it was pitch black so using the candles we had no option but to set our bed up and a single one for the boys to share. We had chips from the chippy and an early night. Because it was a Friday, we had to wait all weekend like this until Monday morning. On the Monday morning, Ian had to go back to work so I was on my own with the boys. It was still snowing and we were freezing. I went to the phone box and rang the electric and the gas to get connected. They both turned up later that day but both said that the house was coming up on their system as being condemned and it would blow up if they even tried to connect us up. That was a bitter blow. No Electricity, No Gas and no water. Plus no toilet!! There was nothing for us to do except make the best of it, which we did for four months. We used candles for light, and a small blue calor gas bottle with a single burner on top to heat up cans of soup and beans etc. we used a plastic bucket for the toilet and went round the corner to the Park and, for a penny, were able to do a 'Number Two'!! During the weekdays, Ian was at work, so Id take the boys down to the only arcade open on the Prom (it was winter!!) and play bingo for hours. It wasn't money bingo but prize bingo and I won loads of stupid toys and tat. I also spent a lot of Ian's wages, and, as we mostly lived on things from the Chip Shop, so we very quickly ran out of money each week. I took to selling our possessions, the ones we didn't need in our one room at the house. Even the boy's toys got sold, with us keeping only a load of small cars for them to play with.

CHAPTER 12

We survived for 4 months in the condemned house in Bank Street, Herne Bay, Kent. At the time, the government offered you 400 pounds if you had been out of work for so long but relocated to another area for work. You had to have been settled for a month and when our month was up it was time for our four hundred pound cheque to arrive. As Ian was earning nine pounds a week, four hundred pound made us feel like millionaires!! The day our cheque arrived we danced and danced around our little room. It was as though we'd won a million dollars. We d never even heard of such an amount. Now that we had such great wealth the world was our oyster. I saw an ad in the local paper for a new house in a development an hour away that needed 400 pounds deposit. We thought that it was meant to be, so arranged to go and meet the Agent at the building complex one day after Ian had finished work. It was an hour away by bus and we had to go down to the prom to get the bus. On the day, when we got to the Bus Stop, we found that we'd just missed a bus and the next one was an hour away. Something, I don't know what, made me suggest that we walk up to the top end of the Prom to the Men's Boarding House we d stayed in when we'd first arrived in Herne Bay, to see if there was any mail for us, as I hadn't thought of checking before. As it happens, 4 years earlier, at aged 17, we had applied to emigrate to Australia. We had seen an Ad in a local railway station that there was going to be an Australia Day Expo in Manchester the following Sunday. So we went and were so impressed that we did everything possible to apply. There had been nothing in England to stay for and it seemed like the opportunity of a lifetime. We wanted the sun, the beautiful houses, the schools for the boys, the beaches and the kangaroos. We were given lots of Application Forms and we went home and filled them all in immediately. After we'd applied, Australia House had told us to wait a few years until we were older and apply again. So we had applied again just before moving to Herne Bay and hadn't thought much about it. When we arrived at the Men's Boarding House that fateful day, there was a letter on the hall table for us, a letter from Australia House telling us to go for our medical check. Back then, if you got as far as the medical stage you were almost guaranteed to go to Australia. Well, all thoughts of buying the new house were gone and we booked our medicals for a few days later. We sorted out what we thought we'd need to take from our small amount of belongings and waited. I bought new underwear for us all for the occasion and we eventually had, and passed our medical. At the same time, we received a letter from Herne Bay Council informing us that they were aware we were living in the condemned house and that we would have to move out within 48 hours. When I rang them to see if this could be extended, while we waited to hear about Australia, I was told that the children and myself would have to go into a Half Way House and that Ian would have to look after himself!!! We decided to go back to Birkenhead and stay with my mum on the Woodchurch Estate while we waited, but this didn't work out, so after one night there we found a caravan in Prestatyn, North Wales, to rent. Even though we knew Australia was a possibility, I'm ashamed to say we spent almost all of our 400 pounds on a portable TV for the caravan, I played bingo in the many arcades in Prestatyn and we went into Pontins Holiday Camp for the day, where

Ian had found temporary work as a porter. One day, while me and the boys were there for the day, they were filming Holiday On The Buses, with Reg Varney and Wilfred Brambell (Steptoe). We managed to get in the audience scene as extras when they were filming the Ballroom Dancing scene . We were all told to put big smiles on our faces as we would all be shown in the film. For this we were paid with a can of soft drink which they brought round on trolleys. If you ever watch Holiday On The Buses, in the ballroom scene you can just see two tiny spots on the floor on the top right hand side. These spots are my two boys sitting on the floor!!! We never did all get our faces in the Movie!! All the time we waited for Australia House to give us the go ahead. We were in the caravan for about two months when, one Sunday, I decided to ring my Mums neighbour (mum didn't have a phone!!) and, to our delight, I was told a Telegram had arrived for us asking did we want to go by boat or plane to Australia. After ringing Australia House we arranged to fly out on 10th June 1973 from Heathrow. We had already organized our passports and paid our 20 pounds each (We were 20 Pound Poms!!) It never bothered either of us that we were leaving family behind (we had no friends!!!) and couldn't wait to get to

Australia. Ian had applied for, and been guaranteed, a laboring job in Wollongong, New South Wales, with Australian Iron and Steel, and we were to go to a Hostel called, magically, Fairy Meadow. We packed up yet again and took the bus back to Birkenhead, via, Chester, and stayed with Ian's sister Christine. On the night before we were due to leave for Australia we went to North Wales to see Ian's brother Keith and his family to say goodbye. Ian's mum came with us. Keith ran a Pub and while we were sitting in the bar that night and I heard Ian's mum say to him "Well son, you could have done much better for yourself." I found this to be highly offensive and got very upset. Other family members who were also there sympathized with me, as none of them liked his mum and it was a very upsetting night for all of us. And so it was that the next morning, we left Birkenhead to go to Lime Street Station with our 3 and a 4 year old boys, Stephen and Martin, and 3 suitcases (won at bingo!!) and got on the train to London and waived goodbye to England without looking back. We were 21.

CHAPTER 13

On the 10th June 1973 we boarded our Qantas flight from London to Sydney. It was the first time we'd ever flown. How exciting was it!!! Heathrow, at that time, was quite a small Terminal and I can remember it only having one café. We had to wait for quite a few hours before our flight and the boys got bored. However, once on board, there were enough empty seats for us all to have a row to ourselves to sleep. This made the immensely long journey bearable. We stopped off at Ceylon and were given tea samples and were soon landing at Kingsford Smith Airport in Sydney. The long flight wasn't bad for us as we were so excited and happy to be starting a new life, and we'd managed to get a fair bit of sleep. Once through Border Control we collected our 3 small suitcases and made our way out into the Arrivals Hall. Unbelievably we saw a man in full chauffeurs uniform holding a sign saying OLLMAN, our surname. He said he was our driver to take us to Fairy

Meadow Hostel in Wollongong. It was like a dream. Once outside I noticed that the sky was much bluer and seemed to be much higher than the sky in the UK. I also noticed that all the houses were single story (bungalows to us) and the roads were much wider. We had arrived in Australia with $32, about 18 pounds, which was nothing. I worried myself sick about how we would pay for our 'Hire Car' to Wollongong. Our driver, after about an hour, pulled into a mountain top lookout, and down beneath us stretched the sea and the beauty of Wollongong. I was so nervous of how we were going to pay the driver that I felt sick with anxiety so probably didn't appreciate the wonderful view of our new home town. Finally we arrived at Fairy Meadow Hostel (Fairy Meadow is a suburb itself) and the driver insisted on getting our 3 bags out of the boot. When I asked him how much I owed him (with my heart in my mouth) he said "Nothing. The Government has paid for this"!!! I was so relieved I almost cried. The Hostel was made up of rows of metal Nissen Huts, with brick toilet blocks set in rows down the middle. After checking into the office we were allocated Hut number 15a. I was told that the rent was due the day after our first pay day (Ian had got work with Australian Iron and Steel, Wollongong's once famous Steelworks and was due to start in 2 days.) Our Hut had a fold out couch made of plastic and 2 metal single beds in the only bedroom. There was a toilet block outside between 6 Huts. We were given 4 cups, plates, cutlery, blankets and pillows, and one toilet roll. We had to wait till we got paid to buy anything else. As there was a big canteen there where we could have 3 meals a day, so we didn't have to worry. The majority of people on the Hostel were from the UK, with a few from Italy and Greece. Our first pay day came just over a week later when we got $111, more money than we'd ever imagined for a weeks work. We immediately went out and spent the lot!! An electric jug, a radio, groceries, and something we thought we'd never need in Australia: RAINCOATS!! Yes it does rain here!!! We'd thought it didn't!! After we'd been at the hostel for a week a man from a Finance Company knocked on our door offering to loan us $2000 to buy a car, which we snapped his hand off for. We thought we were in heaven!!! We bought a Holden Station Wagon for $1990 on Credit. Our new life had begun.

We lasted 6 months on the Hostel at Fairy Meadow before

finding a private house to rent. Plus Id got pregnant with our third son, Lee. Life was good. Homesickness?? It took 5 years before we started to feel settled but we very rarely felt homesick. Life in Australia was too exciting. Ian was working shift work at the Steelworks and we soon got used to the Hostel Life. It was difficult at times as one day, 500 families from Turkey arrived. They let their children use the sinks as toilets and the menu in the canteen started to provide mostly Turkish foods. However, 6 months after arriving at the Hostel, my Friend, Anne, who had moved off the Hostel and into a house of her own, invited us over to her new house for tea. Just seeing her in her own place, with her own nice china plates and bits and pieces, made me want to move out of the Hostel ourselves. So we rented a 3 bedroom house in the Wollongong suburb of Gwynneville and started to buy cheap bits of furniture, crockery, towels etc., all the things needed for our new home. It was from this house that Lee was born on 11th July 1974. He was 9 lbs 7 oz, a whopper. I adored him from the start. Even though we'd wanted a girl after having two boys, I loved him dearly. We'd laybyed a lovely pram for him a few months earlier and I loved walking him to our local shops. However, as usual, one week we had no money and the only thing I had to sell was Lee's new pram. I think I got $20 for it when it had cost $200. I can remember having to carry Lee everywhere (and he was a huge baby!!) until the next payday when we bought a second hand older style pram. It was never the same!!! After a year, we found the rent on the house was too expensive and we never had any money so we moved into a much cheaper 2 bedroom flat at Keiraville. All three boys shared a room and the space was much smaller than we'd been use to but we were better off financially, or so we thought, until the day came when we had so many bills we couldn't pay. There was only one thing for it: we had to sell the car. We still owed nearly two thousand (with the interest) on it but got only $500 when we sold it. However, it got us out of a fix. We never thought anything of selling the car until the following month when we couldn't make the regular monthly repayment. A few weeks later, two men came to our door at around eight in the evening and said they were there to re-possess the car. We didn't have it. We'd sold it, we told them. We were told we shouldn't have done that as the car was still under finance and they'd have to report us to the police. Weeks went by and we thought they'd forgotten about it then, one late evening, when Ian should have come home off the late shift at the Steelworks, he hadn't returned. I walked to the nearest phone box and rang his work only to be told that Ian had been arrested that afternoon by the police and taken away. With shaking hands, I rang the Police Station who put me through to the Watch house. I was told Ian was being held there and charged under 'False Pretences'!!! After Id had a sleepless night, Ian arrived home mid morning the next day. His boss had posted bail for him. He'd been told he'd get a Court Date soon. So began the anxious wait. A week later we were interviewed by somebody from the legal system and we told them why we'd had to sell the car. On the day of the Court Hearing, we all turned up, Ian, myself and our three small children. Ian was told off by the Magistrate and was given a 12 month Good Behaviour Bond and we were told the Police had realized we hadn't sold the car criminally. What a relief. But we still had the problem of finding the monthly payments which were still owing to the Finance Company. It took us a few years to finally pay that car off. All for the sake of $500!!!

The space in the flat as the boys grew was proving too

small so we rented a 3 bedroom house in Warilla. The two eldest boys started to play football, or soccer as its known in Australia, and went to the local school. One day I saw an ad in the paper for people to plant grasses on the beach to prevent subsidence. The money looked good so I found a child minder for Lee, applied for, and got the job. Because I was the only one there with a car, (We'd bought another, much cheaper one) for some reason I was made 'Ganger'', the boss, of about 20 women. All we did all day was to plant grasses in the sand hills. There was a small hut for us to have our two daily breaks in. It had a long table and a bench on each side. We had a large electric Urn for boiling water to make tea. One day we all sat down on the benches but somebody stood up on my side. The boiling Urn was in the middle of the table. The table tilted and the urn, full of boiling water fell over, all over poor Ivy, who copped the lot all over her lower half. She jumped up, fell backwards, and started screaming. No mobile phones in those days so I, being the only one with a car, had to drive to a phone box and call the ambulance. It was terrible. Something that stays in my mind often. Hearing poor Ivy's screams I cant forget. The ambulance took forever, it seemed, to arrive, and Ivy was taken to hospital. About 2 years later I read in the local paper that Ivy had ben run over and killed while crossing a Zebra Crossing. One day, after Id been at the job for about two months, I went home and got Lee from the child minder. He was crying, as usual, and his nappy obviously hadn't been changed for a long time. I decided there and then to give up the job and concentrate on looking after him at home.

CHAPTER 14

I started playing tennis, something Id never done before. It was summer and it was really hard to get motivated in the heat but I kept going. I lost weight and enjoyed looking after the three boys. Then the unexpected happened. I got pregnant again. I had to stop tennis and deal with the morning sickness all over again. Ian and I went to the Doctor and asked for a termination. I was homesick for England and the thought was there that we might return home, plus we had enough on our hands with the three boys. We were 23. The doctor told us not to be so stupid and to go away and have the baby. We were young and should be able to cope. It was good advice, as on 8th August 1976 our much wanted daughter, Shelby Jayne, was born. I was thrilled from the beginning. On his first visit to the hospital Ian brought me the prettiest tiny pink lace dress for the baby and a bunch of pink carnations and little ceramic pink booties. At first, we'd decided to call her

Shannon Ashley, but a few days after I had her, I was still in hospital (as you were in those days) and a nurse came to see this very young patient who had three boys and now her first girl. When she asked the baby's name, I told her 'Shelby', the nurse said, "You can't call a girl that. It's a boys name!!" I believed her and immediately changed the name to Shelby, the first name to come into my head. And so we now had our perfect family. A few months later we decided there'd be no more children for us and Ian was packed off to the local hospital for a vasectomy!!!

A few weeks before I had Shelby, we'd been given Notice that the owner of our rented house wanted it back for his son to live in. We'd applied a few years earlier for a Government house and when we'd received the Notice to Vacate our house, we'd gone to the Council and applied to be housed. As I was heavily pregnant, we were told that if we had a boy, we'd still only be entitled to a three bedroom house, and the waiting list for those was miles long, but if we had a girl we'd be entitled to a four bedroom house and we'd pretty much go to the top of the list. So the day I got out of hospital with Shelby, we went straight to the Council where we were told there was a house in Koonawarra that was currently being cleaned and that it was ours on the following Friday. A year earlier, we'd bought an Old English Sheepdog, Demita, and decided to breed from her. The day after I had Shelby, she gave birth to nine puppies. So not only did we have a new baby, nine puppies and packing to do urgently, we had to find a way to transport all of our possessions to the new house. Hiring a Removalist to do it was out of the question so we asked a friend who had a trailer. It took us all day and many trailer loads but we finally managed it and moved into the Koonawarra 4 bedroom house, which was to be our home for the next five years.

I realize I haven't mentioned my mother up to now. She'd divorced my dad, who'd gone off with another woman, when I was 20, just before we emigrated to Australia. Shortly after, she met a Scotsman in the pub where she worked and took him home. He never left and was to become her second husband. They only had my two younger sisters still at home, and within a short time, Linda, who was aged about 14, was packed off to a Children's

Home as being too unmanageable. So there was only the youngest, Diane, left at home. Don, my Mums new husband, was a tyrant, an angry Scotsman with a filthy temper, and who ruled with a fist of iron from the very beginning. Being a Scotsman, Don decided that they would go up to Scotland and look for work, as there was non for him in Birkenhead. He was a Lorry Driver but had also worked on livestock farms with cows. Poor Diane, she was pulled from pillar to post. Mum and Don could never settle anywhere. They would find a place to work and live but it never worked out as Don's temper always got him into trouble, so they'd be on the move again. Diane had to keep starting at different schools, and, as with me when I was growing up, she never had a uniform, so stood out and was never able to make friends. After several years of this life, Mum an Don decided they would follow us, and emigrate to Australia. I was able to get Don a job at the local slaughterhouse and they applied for, and got, a Working Visa. However, they didn't want to bring Diane over with them, so asked everybody they could think of back in the UK if they would take her in. Nobody would, so, with mush misgivings, Diane, along with Mum and Don, arrived in Australia in 1976. They were never able to settle down, just like Ian and I, but their lives were much different from ours. They picked fruit, Don drove massive trucks right up to the top of Australia, taking Mum with him, and they joined a travelling Fair, with Mum on the Clowns (where you put the ball ion the moving clown's mouth and win a prize if you get a certain number) and Don on the adjacent stall on the Milk Churns (where you have to throw 3 beanbags into the top of the urn to win a prize). They did this for many years, living out of a caravan and annex. They'd ditched Diane when she was 14, along the way, and made her make her own way in life. One night, while they were fruit picking in Shepperton, Victoria, Diane went to babysit for somebody they had met on the campsite. When she went to go back to Mum and Don's caravan the next morning, she found they had packed up and gone. The people who she'd babysat for took her in and phoned the Police but from then on Diane was on her own. This abandonment affects her to this day. When Don was driving trucks, we lived in Wollongong in New South Wales. We'd get no warning of them coming to visit us but would hear the whoosh of the air brakes outside the house and there they'd be. They only ever stayed a night or two as they had to get back on the road but they never brought presents or gifts for my four children. They were certainly not your typical grandparents. Finally, after many years on the road with the fruit picking, the Fair and truck driving, Mum and Don decided to 'settle down' and rented a house in Queensland, amazingly, close to Diane, who had married a Queensland boy and had 3 children. Incidentally, when Diane was getting married, my Dad had just not long arrived in Australia. He went up to Queensland on the coach, a 24 hour journey, in his favourite, and only, pair of pants, which were cream, creased and stained pants to attend her wedding. He took his only other clothes with him, a navy blue suit, and he wore that on the wedding day. You may not know it but it gets really hot in Queensland and the humidity is very high and my Dad was a prolific 'sweater'. He came back down to Wollongong to us on the train and Ian and I went to meet him, Ian in his Air Force uniform. My dad came off the train and I thought "God help the poor people who had sat, for 24 hours, around him on that train. He had on the crumpled and stained cream pants and absolutely stunk of sweat. He had a shirt on that had been long sleeved but he'd cut, very jaggedly, the sleeves off. What a sight he was. However, in Diane's wedding photo he looks very dapper in his suit!!!

CHAPTER 15

With our family complete, we settled down to a normal life, in Wollongong. Money was always a problem and we could never make ends meet. Every payday, we would go to Coles and do our grocery shopping, pay our bills and have very little money left to last us for the rest of the fortnight. So Ian would go to our local garbage tip every Saturday and Sunday and scavenge for things which we could sell. Over the course of five years he brought home televisions, radios, clothes, ornaments and lots of other thrown away things. Every Monday saw us down in Wollongong shopping center at the pawn shop or the second hand shops trying to sell what he'd found. This small amount of money was a godsend. Some weeks he'd come home with nothing and Id be devastated. One day he came home with a locked cash box. After a bit of prising with a screwdriver, it opened. Inside was an old World War 2 Identity Card, Nazi Cufflinks, a gold and ruby caterpillar broach and five gold rings. As Ian had found this tin at the tip, it never occurred to us to hand it in. Naturally we sold all the gold and the broach and handed the rest of the things into the Police. With the proceeds of our sale we were able to take the four children on our first ever holiday, a week in the Snowy Mountains. Not having the money to buy ski outfits, I went to our local second hand clothes shop and bought a motley collection of coats, pants, gloves and hats. With the money from our cashbox find, we rented a small wooden hut an hour away from the snow. On the way there, we stopped at a town called Goulburn for lunch. I had curried sausages (YUK!!) and by the time we'd arrived at our rented cabin a few hours later, it was obvious I had food poisoning. Ian lit the log fire and I got into bed. He then took the four children to see the snow while I ran to the toilet every ten minutes. The following day I felt much better and went with them to Thredbo to see the wonderful vista of the Snowy Mountains. We built snowmen and rode toboggans, rode up on the chairlift and had hot chocolate. We had a great time and we would never have another holiday all together again.

Back home I started to play Competition Squash. Squash in Wollongong had just taken off and there were Squash Courts being built in almost every suburb. Amazingly I never got beaten for two years but it made me terrified of losing and I felt sick when I woke up on competition days, wondering if this was to be the day I lost. Eventually I got beat and I took it really badly. I gave up squash for a few months and listened to classical music to relax me. I went back and started to coach the juniors and slowly began playing again. Eventually, I didn't mind loosing. Ian was sick of the shift work and of driving an overhead crane at the Steel Works so decided to change jobs. He found work at a fiberglass Pool Manufacturers. When he came home every afternoon, you could feel the fiberglass on his skin. One day, around lunchtime, he pulled up outside the house in the old work truck, saying he had to pick up something from Sydney, an hour and a half away each way, and would myself and the baby, Shelby, like to go with him for the ride. You bet I would!!! Anything to get me out of the house. As long as we were back for 4pm when the boys got home from school. I dropped what I was doing and me and Shelby jumped in the front seat of the truck - no baby capsules back then!!! We got to Sydney and did what we had to do, then stopped off for a milkshake. Driving back along the approach road to home 4 hours later, I suddenly went as sick as a parrot. I remembered that just before I'd left the house at lunchtime Id put a chicken in the oven, ON HIGH " to get it going" but hadn't turned the oven down. Approaching our road I imagined fire trucks outside a burnt down house but no, what I did find was black smoke pouring from the windows and my 3 poor boys standing outside not knowing what to do!!! Needless to say the chicken was non existstant and it took us weeks to get the black smoke off the walls. And all for the sake of a run out to Sydney!!!!

After 5 years at that house Ian had been out of work for two of them (he'd been made redundant from the Pool Manufacturers and hadn't been able to get another job). He'd wanted to join the Royal Australian Air Force years before but I'd said no. I didn't want to have to live by myself with the children while he went away. But life was becoming hopeless with him out of work. We had no future, so one day I said to him 'Why don't you apply for the Air Force". He did, that afternoon and, after passing his medical and giving up his lifetime habit of smoking, he joined up in September 1981. The morning he got on the train to Sydney to join up I cried my eyes out for hours. I was to cry almost every day of his three month basic training. Since meeting at 14 and marrying at 16, we hadn't been apart once, apart from the week he first went down to Herne Bay for his new job. Having no mobile phones in those days we couldn't keep in touch and we only had a few phone calls to our public phone box during the twelve weeks. I continued to play squash, sometimes with swollen eyes as I'd been crying for him for hours before. His Basic Training in South Australia lasted 12 weeks. I wrote him a letter every single day, telling him about life at home. Me and the kids even managed to get on an Air Force flight and went down for a day to see him in South Australia. Once he'd finished Basic Training we were then posted to Canberra, Australia's Capital City. We didn't know it then but our lives would change for good.

Our move to Canberra was to change us into what we Brits would call 'Middle Class'. Canberra was like a different world. Because it's the National Capital it is pristine, with beautiful big buildings and a large lake. And most people had a job, mainly in the Public Service. We took the first rental house we saw, a newish small 3 bedroom house in a new suburb, Florey. On Ian's first day at work in the RAAF, he came home and we decided to walk to our local shops for dinner. Ian still in uniform, took off his hat and tie and we went to our local shopping center. In the supermarket, we were halfway up the first aisle and a man in full RAAF regalia comes up to us and blasted Ian for bringing the RAAF into disrepute!!! He tore strips off him for not wearing his uniform correctly!!! Ian and I were devastated. We obviously had a lot to learn. Shelby started school and the boys went to a private Catholic School. We spent 6 months in that small pokey house. During that time we would learn that the RAAF had allotted us a 5 bedroom house as we had 3 boys and 1 girl. Unfortunately (or fortunately for us!!) they didn't have any 5 bedroom houses on their books so they told us to go on to the open rental market and find something ourselves. Of course, we did. We found a massive 5 bedroom, 3 bathroom, house, with a pool, in one of Canberra's southern suburbs. Compared to what we'd been use to it was a mansion. Also, because Ian now had a secure job, we were able to get credit and bought new furniture. I remember our new lounge was L-Shaped, brown with peacocks on it (it was the 80s!!) We thought we'd won the lotto. At this time my dad decided to come over, initially to visit. He had no ties back home and he and my mum had divorced. When he arrived he was very disheveled from the long flight. Unfortunately he decided to remain disheveled. From the first day he arrived I kept saying "why don't you have a nice shower". He'd reply "No I'm Ok for now." After a few days he hummed. It was summer and a sweaty time!!! Plus he wore the same clothes he'd arrived in. His pants were cream but very creased with all stains on them. They were terrible. Finally one day I persuaded him to have a swim in our pool. My neighbor, who was with us at the time, said, "Throw him a bar of soap"!!! While he was in the pool I got the dreaded cream pants and put them in the wash. He was furious as his only other pants were suit pants and he had to wear those until his cream ones were done. On our first proper shopping trip after he arrived I bought him 2 pairs of shorts but he never wore them, preferring his cream pants or his suit ones. One day, coming home from Squash with a friend, I was mortified to see the bedroom window open (our house was single storey) and my dads yellowing underpants hung over the window frame!! He'd washed them and hung them out to dry!!!

CHAPTER 16

For some unknown reason, I hadn't worked since arriving in Australia 8 years ago, apart from the short stint planting grasses on the beach. Now, with all the four children at school, one day I saw two adverts in the local paper that attracted me. One was for Nursing Training at The Canberra Hospital and the other for Mature Aged Entry into the Australian National University in Canberra to do a Degree. After much consideration, I rang the hospital and found out that there was more to Nursing than just sitting on the edge of a bed, stroking a sick patient's hand!! I think it was when the 'bottom wiping' bit came up that I decided it was not for me. Now what made me think I'd stand any chance of getting into the ANU to do a Degree I don't know as Id left school at 14 without a single qualification. The Ad said that you had to go to the University on a certain date and take a 3 hour test in the morning and write a 3 hour Essay in the afternoon. I thought Id give it a crack so turned up at the allotted time and was faced with hundreds of other hopefuls wanting to get into the prestigious University. The first 3 hours were multiple choice questions and I had no idea of how Id done. A lot of the questions I had just guessed at. The second part was easier as it was multiple choice essays. I wrote my essay on how we migrated to Australia and the difficulties we'd faced in settling. My aim, at that stage, was to do law as Id always fancied being a lawyer. We had to wait quite a few weeks before the results were known: When they were announced, I'd got in to do an Arts Degree. So the following March I became a Uni Student. All the kids were by now at school and my Dad was still with us to help look after them. I did Medieval History, Fine Art, Australian History and French. I really enjoyed the work and thought I was breezing through it, so at the end of the first Semester I relaxed. Until I got my first results. I'd failed every subject apart from French, where I'd got 51 per cent. I felt like giving up but that 51 per cent kept me going and I re-wrote all the failed Essays again, this time passing them. When the Christmas break came around I was offered a job as a Property Manager which I thought I could take until Uni started again in March. However, I got too used to the money, a thousand dollars a fortnight, and never went back to Uni. My long life as a Property Manager had started and all thoughts of Uni forgotten. I found the job very hard at the beginning. I had never been a Property Manager before (I'd blagged my way into the job by saying I'd done it before!!) and had 240 properties, worth millions of dollars in my care. I had to first of all get properties onto our books, do an Inventory and type it out (no computers yet!!) advertise the property, interview then chose suitable tenants, do inspections of the properties and follow up on any late or non payment of rents. It was very hard, especially for someone with no experience. However, I soon settled in and made friends of the other staff and Managers. They were very good to us and once a fortnight, on the Friday, they would take us all out for lunch, lasting until 3 or 4 O'clock and on the alternate Friday us girls all received a big bunch of flowers. Those were the days when all this could be written off on Company Tax. That stopped a few years later. At home, my dad had a bad heart problem and had nowhere to go back to in England so I had fought with Immigration for him to stay in Australia. After two years of fighting and many letters telling him he had to leave the Country by a certain date, we were successful at last and he got permanent residency. While I was at work, and the children at school, he would go to the main Shopping Mall in our area and sit in different Café's all day drinking cups of tea and eyeing up the women. He was only in his fifties and liked the ladies. (Remember his days at St Anselms!!) Eventually, after living with us for 4 years, he met a lady friend called Fay and after a few weeks of courting he moved in with her. They had a very tumultuous relationship but married after a few years. They argued constantly, mostly over Religion I later found out. Many a time I would get a phone call from him, usually late at night, asking me to come and pick him up as he and Fay had yet again had a massive row. He'd go back to her in a day or two and make up but this became a habit and Ian and I got sick of it. On the day he died, 30th May 1990, of a Heart attack while eating his jelly and custard, I wailed like a banshee. He'd become like a child to me, with his constant need to be rescued from his tumultuous relationship. I cried for a year and, for some unknown reason and for the first time in my life, wrote poetry. I felt that my Dad was still very close by and talked to him in my head often. When I'd gone to see him in the Funeral Home, I'd cut a lock of his hair and put it in a silver locket.

This locket was to become my talisman for many years.

Ian was still in the RAAF, I was a Property Manager in an up market suburb of Canberra, Manuka. We had a good steady income, although we could never manage to save anything, nor did we buy a house, as the rent the RAAF was charging us was very cheap. And we still had the lovely house with a swimming pool. Life went on. We had been living in Canberra since 1981, quite the middle class life. The boys and our daughter were at Private Catholic Schools and I'd started working as a Property Manager in a Real Estate Agents. That first job I got, I was tipped off by a friend who worked at an Employment Agency. I was told to only tell them about my two eldest boys, who were 12 and 13, and not my youngest two children, as the Real Estate Agency wanted someone who wasn't going to take school holidays off if they had younger children, and had been looking for someone suitable for quite a while. So that's what I did and never mentioned Lee and Shelby, who were 6 and 8 at the time. I worked at that Real Estate Agency for 3 years and made great friends with some of the people there, even having them over to our house for dinner on many occasions, with them all still thinking I only had the 2 bigger boys. When anyone came round to our house for dinner the 2 youngest had to hide in their bedrooms all evening!!! I was particularly friendly with the other Property Manager, Pat. She and I were inseparable. After almost 3 years of our working together, I decided to tell her about the other two children. It took tremendous courage for me to do this as we were so close but I realized I had to do it. To say she was shocked was an understatement. She wouldn't believe me. The news soon got round at work and I noticed a slight difference of attitude towards me. Plus, as was to always be the case, I was getting bored. It was time to move on. Having given my Notice, I left on the Friday and found another job, also in Real Estate as a Personal Assistant to the State Manager of a large Real Estate Company in Canberra, on the Monday. My job was to cater to his every whim. He was a big man, both physically and in personality and a very funny man to work with. On my first day there, he called me into his office and held up a massive pair of suit pants, ripped from one end of the crotch to the other. He asked me if I would take them over to the men's outfitters across the road and have them repaired. When I asked him how it had happened, he said he'd "farted the arse out of them!!!" I had just come from a job in a really upmarket suburb, working with upmarket people in an upmarket Estate Agency, so this man was totally different and to say I was shocked is an understatement. Yet again, after only a short time, I got bored with nothing substantial to do. I had so little to do at this job, answering the phone, making him his cups of coffee and his diet meals in the microwave, and especially after the hard work I'd been used to, that I found it totally unfulfilling. While here though, I did meet a lovely young lady, Deidre Armstrong. Deirdre was only in her late 20's when she found out she had a brain tumor. She'd had small tumors cut off all over her body for years, but her Doctor had said that as long as the tumors stayed away from her Organs she would be OK. But then it hit her brain. Her mother had died, at the same age that Deidre was then, of the same thing. After Chemo she lost her hair and I went with her to the Canberra Hospital Wig Department. She was so appalled by the old fashioned selection of wigs that she refused to wear one and spent the next, and last, year of her life either bald or with a bandana on. Deirdre's Cancer eventually spread to her bones, her spine, and, at the age of 31, died. She was a wonderful friend to me and I still miss her 30 years later. Being bored, and being me, I decided to look for another job. I interviewed, and got, the job, with no experience, of Executive Director (I know, how???) of the YWCA of Canberra. Even though I was The Boss, I answered to a Board of Directors and my first job there was to move the organization into a big house in Manuka, get a new exterior sign made and furnish a new boardroom. I also had to manage the YWCA's financial investments, (it was over a million dollars!!) something Id never done before. Every three months, I would have to find the best bank interest deal and put their money into a short term deposit. I must be a quick learner as I soon was able to do this very easily. Incidentally, Interest Rates back then where up to 17 % where now in Australia they are under 2%. I found out quite quickly that I am not 'The Boss' type as I wanted to be everybody's friend. I had an enjoyable year there but It was very difficult working with so many different personalities of the Board of Directors and I was soon very unhappy.

It was at this time that Ian was posted to Richmond in NSW with the RAAF. We didn't want to leave our cushy lives in Canberra but had no choice. By this time both Stephen and Martin had left school and home and were working so we only had Lee and Shelby to think about. We found a house to rent in Richmond, which was much more down market than Canberra, and put the children in school. I hated it from the beginning. The house was sandwiched in between two blocks of Units and the rowdy young people, especially groups of young men, who lived there made life impossible. The were drunk, it seems like, almost every night and had parties and noisy gatherings. It was so different to what Id been used to in Public Service Canberra, the Nations Capital. As a Property Manager, I applied to the only Real Estate Agency in town but they had no vacancies so, having to earn an income I enquired at the Nursing Home down the road. Now, I've never in my life worked at a Nursing Home or had anything to do with the caring professions, ever. But I was taken on and told to report at 7am the following day. This I did and after being shown where to put my bag I was led to a desk and introduced as NURSE OLLMAN. I quite liked the sound of that. But then I was told to go and shower Mr. X then work my way along the rooms showering all the men there. Me? Shower a man? I was shaking in my boots. Another nurse was sent with me to show me the ropes and Mr. X was wheeled in with his pyjamas still on. "OK" said my trainer", "Take his Pyjamas off, then you can shower him all over then when he's dry dress him in the clothes that are out on his bed." Then she left me. Alone. With Mr. X. Poor Mr. X. Seeing the look of horror on my face, he said to me "Is this the first time you've done this?" I had to acknowledge that yes it was. After taking off his pyjamas, looking away as I removed his bottoms, I had to place a flannel over his bits as I was mortified. The poor man. I hosed him down, front only, and in seconds, with the hand held shower and made him dry himself. I pushed him back into his room and dressed him best I could. As I was helping him dress I heard a shout. "NURSE OLLMAN, NURSE OLLMAN. COME QUICKLY". Another nurse ushered me towards a room where the most almighty smell of faeces was coming from. The man in the room had dirtied himself and had wiped it all over the wall, the bed bars and the blankets as well as all over himself. I was expected to go into the room and help the two other nurses already there to clean it up. I'm ashamed to say I stood in the doorway, heaving, and couldn't go in. I was told by an angry Senior Nurse to go on kitchen duty for the rest of the shift. At lunchtime, I went home and cried. I never went back. OK. So Nursing's not for me. I did managed to find a job as a Property Manager in another town half an hour's drive away. Shelby and Lee were not happy at school. The Public School they were at was very different to their Private Schools in Canberra. Ian didn't mind it so much as he was doing the same sort of job he'd done in Canberra, but after a short while, I hated Richmond so much that I asked to see the RAAF Chaplain at the RAAF Air Base where Ian was stationed. I requested that he use any influence he had to have us moved back to Canberra at the end of the Posting Year. This he did, and after Christmas in 1988 we packed up yet again, and moved back to Canberra.

CHAPTER 17

We arrived back in Canberra in 1988 after our year in Richmond. I applied for, and got, a job selling the Yellow Pages in Canberra, again something I'd never done. I, along with a handful of other recruits were flown to Sydney for 5 weeks, flying home every weekend, to learn how to sell, price, and design the ads. We were put up in a harbourside apartment under the Harbour Bridge and given huge amounts of money (or so it seemed to me back then) for food and living expenses. All of our flights were paid for, plus we got a good weekly wage. I couldn't believe my luck. I felt as though Id hit the big time. Most of our days in Sydney were spent around a big table being taught the different fonts and sizes of the Ads allowed in the Yellow Pages. We were also motivated with the fact that the cream of the crop each year in selling would get an all expenses paid trip. Naturally I never saw myself as one of those people. In fact I was so shy (yes me!!!) for the first time in my life, to even ask questions or make any comment during our lessons. I later found out that the Training Manager rang the Canberra Manager and told him I'd never make it. When the five weeks were over we all turned up at the Canberra office on our first Monday morning, heads filled with sizes, lettering, fonts and the like. We were given two big cardboards boxes with hundreds of sheets of paper in them. On each sheet were the details of all the people in Canberra and surrounds who had a Business Phone and whether or not they had an Advert in the current Yellow Pages (We were selling for the next years' Book). Our job was to pick out a piece of paper and phone the business person on it and try to either sell him any kind of ad in the book or to upgrade his existing one to a bigger better ad, which would cost much more money and go towards out weekly target. The company that ran Yellow Pages, Edward H O'Brien, had introduced a new money making incentive, making the advertiser's Ad stand out with the addition of RED. So even if the advertiser was happy with his existing Ad and didn't want to make it bigger or put another Ad in another section, you could 'Sell Up' by trying to get them to add some red to their Ad. It was to be a good earner for me. The first few calls were really difficult and I stumbled across my words many times but after a while it became easy. I developed a 'patter' which made calling people I'd never met before quite easy for me. I know most, if not all, of the other new recruits struggled for quite a few weeks before they were confident enough. While all the others were sorting their boxes out into sections, I made a start on ringing my leads straight away and made appointments to go and see some of them. You could get a mixed response to your calls with "I don't think the Yellow Pages brings me any business" to "I've been waiting for you to call. When can you come and see me??" Amazingly, one of my first calls greeted me with open arms. "I've been waiting for you to ring. I missed the last Yellow Pages and want to go in the next one." When I went out to see him, he put in THREE large Ads, all with red in them. I was ecstatic and I think that gave me the confidence for the future. And so it was that for 9 months, as I worked on the 1989 Canberra Yellow Pages, my confidence increased more and more and I found that I had a natural affinity with the business people and was able to get plenty of ads from them. At one stage the office introduced a bell to be rung by anybody who had managed to sell a big Ad. I sold at least one a day and was too embarrassed to ring the bell as Id noticed in the beginning much raising of eyes whenever Id got a big order, which was often. Every Friday we had an Office Meeting where the weeks best performer was awarded a crystal glass. Once you'd collected 6 glasses you got the matching wine carafe. How embarrassing was it for me to be almost always the recipient. A collective sigh from everybody and more rolling of eyes were endured. I asked the Office Manager if these weekly ceremonies could be stopped but was told no, as they acted as motivation for the others, something I knew not to be true. What people didn't realize was that I worked extremely hard and was under immense stress to keep it up. I would go out at night till all hours to sell an Ad to a bathroom tiler, or a builder or a restaurant manager. Id fall into bed at midnight after doing my paperwork only to have to be in the office by 7.30 the following morning to get the edge on all the others. Luckily, Ian was wonderful and looked after the kids, who were by this time either left home or were in their teens. At the end of the campaign I was number one in the whole Company, which stretched right across Australia. At that time, the trip for those who'd done well was to Ayers Rock and the Northern territory, but there was an airline pilots strike on in Australia. It was announced to the chagrin of the others, that instead, this years trip would be to Hawaii!!! You could take a partner with you, all expenses paid. We paid for Lee and Shelby to come with us as I'd earned so much money in commission that year. Naturally the Trip was fantastic and at the end of the Hawaii leg we could still afford to go over to Paris and England as well. All in all, my year at Yellow Pages was a very fruitful one but one that would burn me out and make me not want to work anymore. After a wonderful month long holiday, we returned just after Christmas and in the New Year our whole Team were sent down to the Coastal area of Batemans Bay to do their Yellow Pages. But I was burnt out. I had no inclination to sell Ads anymore. Having been the Company's top seller in Canberra the previous year, there were great expectations of me. I hated it. But I had to make money so I kept going until I found yet another job, this time at at WIN TV, Canberra's local TV Station. Again this was selling Advertising (my title was Advertising Executive, which I loved!!!) but I was also able to help with the Production of making the Ads, which I really enjoyed doing. I started to take a little make up bag to the shoots when we filmed the Ads, and apply a bit of face make up to those people who would appear in them. It made me feel very important, and I decided to apply for a job in Production as an Editor. This job proved to be a lifesaver as there was almost no stress and a very easy product to sell (who doesn't want to be on tele!!!) I really enjoyed my time at WIN TV. I was quite successful there and mostly made my monthly target. But memories of our trip to England had me buying Country Life Magazines and soon Ian and I were pining to go back and live there, to move back to the England we'd envied so much in the wonderful countryside pictures, with the thatched cottages and rolling hills. But then, on 30th May 2000, a bolt of lightening struck. My precious dad died of a heart attack.

CHAPTER 18

My dad dying was probably the single most disastrous thing that had ever happened to me in my life. I Couldn't function for months after his death. I was lucky that WIN TV allowed me as much time off as I needed but I was devastated. My dad had almost been like my child. I'd helped him through a very difficult marriage, had him stay with us when things went wrong at home and generally looked after him. However, Ian and I decided that we still wanted to go back and live in England, taking with us our two youngest children, Shelby and Lee, who were then 14 and 16 years old, a terribly crucial time in their education, but we thought we could overcome that. So at the end of 1990, in December, I said goodbye to WIN TV, Ian left the RAAF and we sold everything we had apart from some boxes of photos and mementoes, and moved back over to England. But not to Birkenhead. During all the previous months of planning, Ian had noticed there were quite a few

IT related jobs (IT was his profession in the RAAF) in Leeds, so we rented a beautiful old cottage on the York/Leeds Road. Unfortunately nothing came of the Leeds jobs so we moved into a house in York. I immediately found work at a free weekly newspaper as a Telesales Marketer, selling in the Public Notices and Job Vacancies section. I found this very easy after having worked so hard on Yellow Pages in Australia and stayed there for six months. Ian found a job at RAF Base, Linton on Ouse, half an hour outside York, working in the supply squadron. At my job, I got a call one day from a man saying that they were looking for an Advertising Sales Executive for Yorkshire Life Magazine and could he put an Ad into the paper. I was very tempted by this job, as, yet again, I was bored and unfulfilled in my job, and I felt it was right up my street. I, as always, had my CV with me in my desk drawer so faxed it straight to him. He never put the Ad in the paper and I started the following week without even an Interview. This time though, there was a bit of a bonus. I got a Company Car. I was responsible for the advertising in the magazine for the whole of North Yorkshire and worked from home, going into the office 2 hours drive away in South Yorkshire, once a month for a

Meeting. The job couldn't have been more perfect. The only problem was we had to work to a monthly Target of 9,000 pounds. This was very hard to make as the Ads were so expensive (It, and it's Sister Magazines were, and are to this day, upmarket Magazines). I was lucky though and managed to reach this Target most months, albeit in a mad rush on the last few days of each month. One day I realised that, as I worked alone in North Yorkshire, nobody was writing any pieces on landmarks and villages or doing Hotel and Restaurant Reviews in my area. Other sister magazines did have people doing this so I could do that I thought. I rang our Editor and asked if I could do it. She said yes, why not. She'd give me a go and see what my writing was like. That was the beginning of my writing career with Yorkshire Life. I got to interview Michael Palin, Mik Kaminski, the violinist from ELO, and numerous hotel Managers and Chefs and posh shopkeepers. Ian and I would go to a different Hotel every week, have a FREE Dinner, Bed and Breakfast then Id write 1500 words about it for the Magazine , all good of course as we wanted them to advertise with us. You wouldn't believe it but after we did half a dozen posh hotels, Ian would moan "Do we have to go"!!! One day, after Id been selling and writing for

Yorkshire Life Magazine for about a year or so, I rang a Wedding Reception venue called The Boat House to put an Ad in a Wedding Special the magazine was having. The girl I spoke to who answered told me that Sir Michael S. owned The Boat House and that she was leaving due to illness. She told me she was Sir Michael's Personal Assistant. I can do that I thought, as usual, and got Sir Michaels details off her. I immediately emailed him asking for an interview. 3 days later I got a call from his wife Lady S. asking me to come and see Sir Michael that Sunday. My oh my!! When we went on Sunday it proved to be a whole Estate, complete with Georgian Mansion and Staff Cottages as well as The Boat House. I wasn't in the least bit nervous sitting in the grand Library in front of a log fire with a very haughty Sir Michael, who asked me a thousand questions. I must have impressed him as he asked me to go along the following Saturday to do a typing test. Now that did worry me a bit as I'm not the best typist but along I went and was given the choice by the Estate Manager of using the electric typewriter or the computer. COMPUTER!!!! Nobody said anything about a computer (it was only 1993). I didn't even know how to turn it on so I opted for the typewriter. I made so many mistakes and had to start again and again that eventually Sir Michael himself came to see where I'd got to. Amazingly, after reading my typing Sir Michael offered me the job saying that a riverside cottage came with the job. I was over the moon. We moved into the cottage and my job as Personal Assistant and Boat House Manager had begun. Yet again, I was to have another new job and another new career.

We moved to the large Estate in North Yorkshire, in a beautiful tranquil village with stone cottages lining a babbling stream. Our cottage was given to us as part of my employment as Personal Assistant to Sir Michael, a Baronet, and his wife Lady S. I was also to be the Manager and booker of The Boat House , a beautiful glass fronted building used mostly for wedding receptions. Now bear in mind Id never done anything like this before and Sir Michael was a typical toffee nosed aristocrat, it was a quick learning curve for me. Sir Michael and his wife spent quite a bit of time down in their London home so I would be left with just the housekeeper and houseman. Once I'd finished my daily work, we would all go into the big kitchen and chat for hours. Sir Michael and his wife would often be gone to London on a Monday morning by the time I started work at 9am, and in my office in his Georgian Mansion (which was the old flower room!!) he would leave big piles of paperwork with different coloured Post it Notes on top of each pile, red ones being urgent and so on. We worked by Dictaphone and he would also leave a tiny tape on top of each pile. The work was very varied. One that sticks in my mind is his voice through the Dictaphone saying "Trish, a note to my wife in these terms: Darling, please do not buy Darjeeling tea from Fortnum's in future. I much prefer Harrods own brand". I would have to type this, then copy it twice, one copy for Sir Michael, a copy for his wife and a copy for my file to prove Id done it down the track if challenged. Another note was : "Trish, (angry voice bordering on apoplexy) Whose is that bloody car that was parked near the Boat House Archway on Saturday. Give them a blast and tell them this isn't a bloody parking lot!!". On investigation I found that the car had belonged to the Lord Mayor of Pocklington who had been attending a Boat House function and had left his driver and car close to the Boat House entrance!! Sir Michael and Lady S had an old retired retainer, Mrs. G, who came in every Wednesday to make butter. She'd been a general servant to the family years before and, as is the habit with aristocrats in the UK, they tend to keep on old retainers, getting them to undertake menial tasks just so they can keep them on the books and pay them a little something. Down in the cellar was a massive chest freezer full of butter that had previously been made by Mrs. G. and it was years old. The butter was made from 2 Jersey cows that were part of the Estates farm and after the milk had been separated from the cream (while Mrs. G coughed, sneezed and smoked!!!) the butter could be made. No salt was added. Lady S. Gave me a pat of it one day and I had to throw it out. It was feral. Vile. I don't know how they ate it. One late afternoon, Lady S came into my office and asked me why the pheasant's she'd ordered from the gamekeeper hadn't arrived. I didn't know so rang the old, surly gamekeeper who told me in no uncertain terms and in very colourful language that Lady S certainly hadn't asked him for any pheasants!!! When this message was passed to Lady S she was very annoyed as they had important guests for dinner that night and said that the gamekeeper had better shoot 6 pigeons and get them to the housekeeper within the hour. On my walk home shortly after, I heard 6 gunshots and thought of the poor pigeons and the poor guests who'd be eating them (Sir Michael would never allow any sauce or gravy and almost everything they ate was from the Estate). The following morning Lady S asked the housekeeper/cook why all the pigeon meat was in the dogs' bowls. She was told that every guest had returned his or her plates with the pigeon meat uneaten, indeed some of the meat still had shot in it!!! Sir Michael was a harridan. I was scared of him but not afraid to stand up to him. The same cant be said of his poor wife who was constantly crying and retiring to her Boudoir (yes, she really did call her study that!!). I was once asked to join them for Christmas Eve lunch. It was to be the full works: pheasant and vegies from the garden. No sauce or gravy. Sir Michael Lady S, their son, their daughter and her husband and 2 grandchildren and me, all perched (me on a stool!!) around the kitchen table for Christmas lunch. Not even the children spoke, not a single word, and it was the most uncomfortable meal I've ever had plus I had to force myself to eat the almost raw pheasant and underdone veggies. At the end of it, Lady S said "OK back to work everyone!!!

CHAPTER 19

I worked for Sir Michael for 3 years, my longest job ever. Working in a large Georgian Country House with the antiques and books and old pictures was all ours when they were in London: Me, the housekeeper Helen and the houseman John. We would gather round the big kitchen table drinking tea and eating homemade cake but always aware that we were there to work. Each days work I did had to be posted to Sir Michael in London every day so I couldn't really slack off too much. Each day a new parcel of work with the dreaded tape was delivered to me from London. It was worse when they were home. There was a terrible atmosphere, everyone was on edge. The Boat House was easy to deal with. All I had to do was to sell it to couples wanting to have their Wedding Reception or Function there, show them round and smile, It was so, so beautiful. It had once been a Riding School for Sir Michael's children but he had converted it into a Function

Centre for his eldest daughters wedding and been persuaded by the Estate Manager to hire it out. Sir Michael did this but never liked the intrusion most weekends. I had to Make sure there was enough staff and organise the Caterer. Ian was still working at the RAF Base at Linton-on-Ouse, about 45 minutes drive away. He was sick of all the travelling so I got him the job of Boat House Manager, and on Event Days, he would go and lay out the tables and tablecloths, candles, flowers etc., make sure the bar was stocked and ready and generally look after the event. It was a long hard day for him as he wouldn't get home until around 3am in the morning.

On our 25th Wedding anniversary, as we had no close friends to have a party, we decided we'd go to Egypt for a fortnight. We flew Egypt Air to Cairo and were bussed out to Giza, where the Pyramids are. We stayed in a crappy 3 star hotel with a dirty green pool but we didn't care. Egypt is the one place where everyone should visit once in their life. It is so unlike anywhere else we had ever seen. On our first morning there, we had a meeting with our Tour Guide and she told us that there would be hundreds of local taxi drivers who would want to take us round. She told us to chose one and stick with him for the whole week, as it would save us a lot of hassle. How right she was. When we first walked out of the Hotel on that first morning the Taxi Drivers were there, crowding around us in throngs. One driver stood out as he started to push all the others away. He said "Come with me to my Taxi and I'll look after you". He took us round the corner of the Hotel and into an alley and to an old wreck of a car with TAXI painted on the side in fading paint. His name was Sabbah and he took out a photo album. In it were hand written testimonials from past customers and he proudly displayed these to us, just as though he was being interviewed for the job. Most said 'Sabbah is a great Taxi Drive. He is very safe" and the like. We got in his taxi and asked to be taken to another, more luxurious Hotel we'd been told about, for lunch. Sabbah said that first he would take us to his brother's shop who sold souvenirs. We said "No, we want to go straight to the Hotel Mena". "No, No, said Sabbah, I take you to brothers. It will only take a few minutes". And that was the start of our week with Sabbah. It didn't matter where we went, or for how long, he always stayed outside, sitting under a tree waiting for us, and fighting the other taxi drivers away, who were ever present, everywhere. We ended up going to his various 'relatives', a perfume shop, a mango farm (where incidentally, we were forced to buy 12 Mangoes on the last day of our time in Giza. They ended up in the bin!!) and back again to the Gift Shop where we finally bought some souvenirs. On our second night in Giza, we were taken to the Pyramids to see The Light Show. Now, Id always thought the Pyramids were on their own in the middle of a desert. They're not. We drove into a town center, heaving with Egyptians and tourists. It was a very dark night. There was a big Stadium type building with booths to pay to get in, just like a Football Stadium. Once in, all in front of us was pitch black. We sat in rows and could see nothing. Egyptian boys were coming round selling bottles of soft drinks and classical music was playing. All of a sudden a booming mans voice came on saying "In The Beginning ….." and a light suddenly comes on, and there, right in front of us, is The Sphinx. It was the MOST amazing sight. After the man's voice gave us the history of the Sphinx (everything else still in darkness), another light comes on and there is the Great Pyramid. Then another. It was magnificent, but so unlike what I'd expected. I thought the Pyramids stood alone in the middle of a desert, not with a town built around them. Hundreds of hawkers were everywhere, trying to sell souvenirs. In the end they became the bain of our holiday.

By 1996 I was still working for Sir Michael. I used to be summoned to Sir Michaels room, The Library, and I would actually stand outside his door for a few minutes building up the courage to knock. I hated it when he was home!! But I got used to it. Then something happened that would once again change our lives. I got RSI (Repetitive Strain Injury) in my left arm from all the typing. After a month or so, I then got it in the right arm from overcompensating, not being able to use the left arm much. Sir Michael was quite good about it and employed a typist to help me out, but because he was so meticulous I always ended up having to correct the typists work. My RSI got worse, in both arms. I taped a thick pencil rubber around a pen and used that to type with, but it didn't really work. I tried injections, physio, acupuncture, nothing worked. So we made the decision to look for other work. Only problem was if I left the job we lost the cottage. Plus we were fed up with North Yorkshire. We'd done a fair bit of travelling in our time but the people there only seemed to want to talk about local things and sheep and cows. After three years there, yet again it was time for a change. Id always wanted to live down South, maybe Devon or Cornwall, so we set about looking for another job. We went for one interview in The Midlands with a Duke and Duchess. When we arrived at their stately home (with deer and peacocks in the Park) the Duke was actually mopping the kitchen floor!!!! They were a lovely couple but wanted Ian and I to supervise the cleaning, and wait at table when they had dinner guests and this we felt we couldn't or didn't want to do. The accommodation offered was a lovely flat at the top of the stately home but as we had a dog and a cat, we couldn't even consider it, so we kept looking.

CHAPTER 20

There's a magazine called The Lady, which advertises live in jobs so we bought that and spotted a job that offered a detached cottage in exchange for a man to garden and the woman to help in the house and with two young girls. We went down to Oxfordshire for the interview and were offered the job on the spot. It was a big 100 year old country house that hadn't been lived in for 25 years, when its then owner, a Saudi Prince, had died from a drug overdose. The house had been sold for 750,000 pounds, was set in 7 acres, with the separate cottage, its own pub, big pool, summer house, stables and tennis court. Everything was very run down, there were masses of cobwebs in the pub (don't forget it had been empty for 25 years!!), which still had the used glasses on the bar and bottles of unopened alcohol on the shelves. The house had come completely fully furnished right down to towels and books. The couple who'd bought it had built up a successful business then sold it for a fortune and bought this Estate. Their plan was to live in the house while It was being upgraded around them. We gave Notice to Sir Michael, packed up yet again and moved to Oxfordshire. At first it was so lovely not to have a Sir Michael to worry about. I cooked meals for our new employers, drove them to the Station if they went anywhere, helped keep the old house as clean as it could be and looked after their two girls after school a few times a week. But after a while we noticed we were being asked to do more and more. Ian had to make a veggie garden from scratch (he'd never gardened in his life!!!) and my workload increased. In my spare time I taught myself to paint on China and to make Papier Mache bowls and teapots. But it never felt right. Cleaning someone else's house and looking after children was not me. After ten months we gave our Notice and rented an old cottage in Dorset, a lovely little village called Buckhorn Weston. Ian had got a job in Bath, about an hour away by train, in a Publishing Company, reviewing Computer Game CDs. He worked 10 days a month which paid enough to keep us. For the first time I wasn't working and decided to lose weight and get fit. In 6 months I'd lost 40 kilos and was riding my bike everywhere. I wrote a TV play with a woman Id met and befriended and started the first chapters of a book (which was never finished incidentally!! Something I've been very good at doing!!) My RSI had disappeared and we were happy doing nothing. However, after we'd been there a year three things happened at once: We got a letter from the owners of the house saying we had to move out as they wanted to use the cottage as a Holiday Home, on the same day Ian lost his job, then we were told our car wouldn't pass its MOT. We'd been in England for 7 years and suddenly going back to Australia seemed a good option. I felt Id rather be poor in Australia than in the UK. We sold some antiques we had (Royal Doulton figurines and China) and booked 3 tickets back to Canberra. We still had our daughter and son who were 23 and 21 with us but our son stayed behind and got a job as a gamekeeper on a big Estate in Dorset. So once again, we sold up all the possessions we had apart from photos and mementos, hired a car for the day and drove to Heathrow Airport. Goodbye England. Yet another new life in Australia awaited!!!

Living back in England wasn't meant to be for us. We loved the television, the sweets, the food and the curry and chips, the history and the countryside, all the stuff we cant get in Australia. But no house, no job and no car didn't bode well and we thought we d rather be poor in Australia than England. So on 21st February 1998 we arrived back in Canberra. We d sent some boxes of photos and Ian's computer over but apart from that we arrived, once again, with just 3 suitcases to our name. Luckily our daughter-in-law's mother had a house with a self contained flat underneath it and she said we could stay there. At this stage I should point out that 6 months earlier, before we had left England, our daughter, Shelby, had developed mental illness and had been hospitalised, so we thought that maybe coming back to Australia might be the boost she needed. She'd also had a nasty accident when she was 17 on her moped, where she'd broken her femur, tibia and fibular. It had taken her two years to walk again, so she was very fragile. The night we got back we went out to eat and we all just looked at each other and, with sinking hearts, said "What have we done!!!". Once again we had nothing. No home, no jobs, no money. However, yet again, luck was on our side and within a fortnight both Ian and I had found work, Ian as a Computer Technician with CSIRO, the Government's Scientific Research Organization, and me as a Property Manager. We found a small house to rent for Ian and I while Shelby stayed at the flat, we bought a dog and a cheap car and second hand furniture. Slowly our lives returned to normal and once again we were Australian.

We d been married for 30 years and we d never bought a house, always rented. As I was working full time we decided we d try and save all my money to put down on a house to buy. Finally, with Shelby's help,(shed got compensation for her Moped accident) we bought our first house. It was $129,000 but it was ours to paint and hang pictures up as we wished. We were in heaven. Our first house of our own after 30 years of marriage. Ian built a pergola out the back and we painted the inside walls to our hearts content. I changed jobs again out of boredom but Ian had cemented himself into his job at CSIRO and was proving to be invaluable. Unfortunately our daughter started regularly being admitted to psychiatric wards and lived with us when she was home. I started working only until 1pm to be able to care for her but if I wasn't home by

1.10pm all hell would let loose as she had waited for me to get home to get her lunch. Many a time I came home only to find her missing then the phone would ring. It would be the hospital telling me they had her there, having taken another overdose!! This went on for some while when, one evening, she came into our room late at night and told me she'd taken another overdose. She insisted on driving herself to hospital but for me it was the final straw. The next morning I rang the hospital and told them she wasn't coming home and they had to find her other accommodation when she was discharged. My life at this point was a nightmare. Living with someone with mental illness has to be one of the worst things ever. I was stressed to the point where I felt physically sick all the time. The hospital found her a place in a refuge and things seemed to pick up. I no longer had to be home by 1pm and found myself a full time job. Shelby and I had both bought a horse each that year and had them aggisted locally. When, in our local newspaper, we saw a large 27 acre block of undeveloped land for sale cheaply, we jumped at the chance and thought it would be good to put a Kit Home on it and have the horses there. It was a fair way out of Canberra but we didn't mind. We put an offer in for the land and put our house on the market on the same day. Our offer on the land was accepted and our house sold 2 weeks later for $80,000 more than what we had paid for it a year ago. Our new block of land was about 45 minutes out of Canberra, in the middle of nowhere on a mountain. It was obviously mountainous and rocky but had a flat house site already dug out, and electricity and phone connected to the bottom of the land, at the gate. We sold most of our furniture and stored the rest of our things in our sons garage and hired a caravan and portaloo and moved out there. It was so quiet and peaceful, although with those pesky kangaroos everywhere, jumping out in front of the car. I'm sorry to say we killed a few that way!! We truly were in the bush. Unfortunately the only downside was that some of our journey back to the highway was on dirt road and this proved to be hard on the car so we bought a heavy duty ute. One of Ian's first jobs was to build a paddock for the horses and they were soon living with us. Stephen, our eldest son, had met and married a lovely girl, Paulina and had our wonderful grandson, Alex. Stephen and Paulina both had good jobs and were very settled in life. Martin, our second, had also met and married Megan and they had three children, 2 boys and a girl. Both boys were

Webmasters, building Websites for the Australian Government and were on good pay. Lee, our youngest son, was working doing farm work, fencing, soldering and the like. He liked the country life and was happy. Shelby had been given a Government Flat and was living with a friend. She still went in and out of hospital but was coping. On the land, while we lived in the caravan, I experienced one morning excruciating back pain and had to go into hospital to have a disc removed. On my first day in hospital a doctor had come in to see me. He was elderly and had a big bulbous red nose. He ordered an MRI then afterwards told me he'd operate the next day. After he'd left my room, one of the nurses came in and asked me what he'd said. When I told her he was going to operate, she said "Oh my God!! Don't let him do it. Get someone else. That's all I can say!!!" When I asked other staff what she meant I was met with a wall of silence so I rang my Neurologist and told him. He said "We never had this conversation but get someone else. Under no circumstances let him operate!!". I then rang another Neurosurgeon and explained my problem to him and he arranged everything for me and agreed to do the surgery. It turned out that the first Doctor was an alcoholic and had the shakes and had left many people in wheelchairs. About a year later he made front page news in The Canberra Times and had been struck off!!! Id had a lucky escape. I was in hospital 8 days and when I went back to our caravan, Ian and my sons had almost finished putting the garage up. They had insulated one side of it and put in a partition wall. We bought an offcut of carpet and made one side of the garage to live in and used the other side as storage. We were without power or water for a while until we could arrange to have the electric brought up to the house site and the new Water tank installed once the shell of the house had been built, but we did have our portaloo. Until then though, we bought 2 large plastic containers and Ian filled them up at the garage every day with water and we bought a generator, which would only let us run 2 things off it at once. Our plan was to buy a Kit Home but somebody told us it would be better to find a picture of a house you liked then take it to an architect and get a house designed. This we did, then found a builder, and thus began one of the happiest times of our life: building our own spectacular home on the mountain. We were to call it Little Mountain.

CHAPTER 21

We settled well into Little Mountain and loved its tranquility. We were living on the top of a mountain, with only the birds and kangaroos for company. We loved it. For the first time in my life I felt as though I might have found somewhere to settle down. In August of 2002, Shelby had a daughter, Jade, whom I worshiped from that moment she was born. Shelby never bonded with Jade so I had her a lot of the time, giving up work to do so. There were half a dozen frightening episodes where Jade, as a small baby and toddler, held her breath until she passed out. It would only last for ten or twenty seconds but was so scary. I'd pick her up from where she'd collapsed and hold her upside down. She'd start breathing again and had no after effects at all. We will never know why she did it! Jade's dad had not stuck around, but however, when Jade was about 6 weeks old, Shelby rang him to tell him he had a daughter. He came to visit her, stayed for 4 days and left again. It was to all of our great shock that Shelby found herself pregnant again. She couldn't cope with her new baby so how was she to cope with another one, we thought. I virtually brought up Jade while Shelby was pregnant and 11 months after giving birth to Jade, Shelby gave birth to a boy, James. Life seemed a nightmare. I'm sad to say that I left Shelby to mostly just get on with raising the new baby while I had Jade. Life went on and the babies became toddlers. Ian and I had the two of them every weekend and three or so nights in the week as Shelby's mental illness had not improved. She regularly went into the Psychiatric Hospital and we'd have the 2 children. Id started working full time again as a Property Manager and Ian was still at CSIRO. Life working full time and looking after two small children was hard. On our block of land, we built a large above ground Pool and did some outside landscaping and made Little Mountain into a glorious home, however there was still that long arduous journey, part on dirt road, and mostly with two little ones to entertain on the long drive.

Ian and I decided to go on holiday after seeing a brochure. It was for two weeks in England and two weeks in Italy. It was wonderful being back in Birkenhead again, seeing all the family, going to Grange Road, The Pyramids and the Market, although I must say that the once famous Birkenhead Market had gone downhill and was almost empty when we were there. We hired a car and drove to York, and saw where we had lived and worked. We drove to Devon and Cornwall and had a few days in London. Then over to Italy where we'd never been before to join up with a Tour Group. There was supposed to be someone at the airport to meet us and take us to our Hotel before starting our Coach Tour. However, at Milan airport, we waited two hours and nobody came. We asked at the Service Desk how to get to the hotel. We don't speak a word of Italian so I showed the man our itinerary and pointed to our Hotel. He told us in broken English to take a bus from outside the airport to the main Railway Station in Milan and then get a taxi. This we did but after ten minutes in the taxi, the driver said "No Hotel Dino here. You get out now." So out we got, pulling our trolley suitcases along the cobbled road. One of my wheels broke off so I had to carry the case. We were in the middle of the city of Milan, thousands of people milling around us, all speaking a language we didn't know. I stopped a man in a suit and asked him if he spoke English. Luckily he did and when I showed him our itinerary he said we were two hours away from where we needed to be. I nearly collapsed in shock as by this time we'd been in Milan for four stressful hours. The man pointed us in the direction of the railway station and told us to get a train to Baverno, where our actual Hotel Dino was. Naturally the large Train Station was heaving with people and we didn't have a clue which train to get on. At the ticket desk I just showed the man our itinerary and pointed to our Hotel. He told me in Italian what platform we needed to be on and I took a guess that he'd said nine. We got on the train there and had no idea how far Baverno was or even if it was the right train. I walked along the carriage asking people if they spoke English. I finally found a teenage schoolboy who did, and he told me that it was about a two hour ride before Baverno. It was a nightmare, just not knowing where we were. After an hour and a half, we got our bags and prepared for every Station to be Baverno. Eventually we got there and stood at the door waiting for it to open. But it didn't. It stayed shut. Ian then had to physically force the door open and get our cases out of a small gap. It was terrible as we didn't know if the train was suddenly going to start up again. Finally we got out and had reached Baverno. We saw a taxi outside the Station and got in and asked for the Hotel Dino. We strapped ourselves in but 30 seconds later, the drive pulled into…. The Hotel Dino. It was almost directly opposite the Station. And he had the cheek to charge us for the journey!!! After such a disastrous start the rest of the Tour went fabulously. We were tourists in Italy and I'll never forget it. We went from The Lakes area, Lake Como and Milan, Venice, Pisa, Florence and Rome. Almost all of our Tour was filled with Americans and, as usual, there is always one loud one. We got him on our Tour. He made our coach journey's hell. But we left Italy feeling like we'd been somewhere really special and I loved it. Back at home, and for the first time, I'd left Shelby on her own with the two small children. She'd managed, but only just. The day after we got back she went into the psychiatric hospital for a month.

CHAPTER 22

After five years in Little Mountain we had tired of the long, daily journey to and from work, so much that we decided to sell up and buy a house in Canberra. Our house sold on the first weekend we put it on the Market, and we made a massive profit. We bought a 1970's house in Canberra desperate for renovation. When we'd gone to view it for the first time the owner proudly told us that the shag pile brown carpet had never been cleaned once since 1976.!!! We Legally Settled on the house and got the keys at 2pm and by 4pm the brown carpet had been torn up and the archways had all been knocked down and made square. There was rubble everywhere but we couldn't have been happier. Using the Builder who I used at work to do maintenance for me, his team put all new down lights in and painted the whole house cream. It looked lovely. You might, by now, be thinking, surely they now decide to settle down, but no. After just a year there, wanderlust once again struck us and the decision was made to move back over to England to live. Once again, we'd been buying The Country Life Magazine and seeing all the beautiful countryside and houses made us yearn to be back home. Shelby wanted to come with us so we put the house up for auction as well as auctioning off everything we possessed apart from photos (which we shipped over). The contents Auctioneers came two weeks prior to the Auction and labeled and numbered all the Lots and on the day came early in the morning and set up their payment desk and display cabinets in the garden. At 11am people were allowed to walk through the house to look at everything for sale. We had been big collectors and had many Prime Minister's signatures and signed First Edition Agatha Christie books so there was a lot of interest. In fact hundreds of people turned up. The Auction started at noon and had finished by 4pm. We even sold our car. We'd hired a car and when the Auction finished people were coming into the house to collect what they'd bought so we decided to go out and have a coffee and leave them to it. We got back at 5.30pm and there was not one solitary single item left in the house. It was completely bare. All's we had to do was wipe down the kitchen and bathrooms and vacuum.

Once again, we were leaving our three lovely boys, who by now had really good jobs and families of their own. They never seemed to mind my wanderlust and always wished us well. We spent the next two nights at a cheap motel and flew out of Canberra for London not looking back, yet again.

Because Jade and James had been born in Australia but had British grandparents, they were given a Residential Visa by The British Embassy, allowing them to stay in the UK indefinitely. Ian, a Computer IT Specialist, was looking for jobs around the Liverpool area but couldn't find anything. He did however see some prospects in Leeds so, our having lived for a while in North Yorkshire, we decided to go back there and see how we got on. We made one huge mistake. We went at the end of November, which was straight out of our summer. To say that it was absolutely freezing beyond freezing is an understatement. We hired a rental farmhouse near Malton, North Yorkshire, and spent 4 weeks going into Tescos or Asda and buying everything that you'd need to start up two households. Not only did we have to do this for ourselves but we had to do it for our

Shelby and her two children, who'd come with us with no money. We'd made a lot of money on the sale of our two houses so money wasn't a problem. Ian and I we bought only the best. Everything from Tea Towels to Lounge Suites. Cutlery to electric cookers. We loved it and it was such a novelty being back in the UK and seeing all the different products we could buy. After a month in the farmhouse, we eventually got a house on a farm for Shelby and the children. It was very rural and bitterly cold. Ian and I found a small house attached to the Estate Office of a large Country Estate, in a tiny hamlet near Malton. We spent a pleasant enough Christmas there as it was all new and exciting and we were able to buy the things we had missed while living in Australia. But as the New Year came, I just knew we'd made the wrong decision. I couldn't cope with the cold and never left the house apart to go grocery shopping. The only aspect I enjoyed of our new life, once the novelty of the shops had worn off, was that one day in March, it snowed. Heavy enough to settle quite deeply on the ground. The children loved it. I loved it. Only poor Ian, who had found a job at a School in York fixing their computers, and who had to drive to work in it, hated it!! Even though we had some money, we found the cost of living to be high. The price of keeping both Shelby and ourselves in Heating Oil was horrendous. Two hundred and fourty pounds each every month. One night, after we'd been there for just 4 months, there was a program on TV about people who had emigrated to Australia, not liked it and gone back to live in the UK but then decided they wanted to be in Australia after all. That was it for me. The following day I rang an airline and booked us all back on a flight to Sydney in two weeks time. Poor Ian never got a choice. My daughter also wanted to come back so we arranged to try and sell our near new belongings. At the time, there were three second hand dealers in the York Yellow Pages. I rang all three in succession. The first one came round and said he'd give us a hundred pounds for the lot (There was about ten thousand pounds worth of stuff!!). The second one said he had too much stock to take on any more but the third one said he couldn't buy it from us but could store it until the next Auction and we'd sell it all that way at a later date. By that stage, we had no option but to do this. Because we'd taken a two year Lease on ours and Shelby's house, we couldn't break them so we had to do a moonlight runner. We did this on a Saturday, although not in the moonlight!! On the big day, I looked out of the window to make sure there was nobody working in the Estate Office only to see dozens of horses and riders. There was a Hunt on. Horses, Riders and Spectators were all gathering outside our house. How would the removal van park to take our things to the storage Unit?? To say that we were nervous that somebody from the Estate Office would come is an understatement. Don't forget, we were doing a moonlight flit. When the large van arrived the driver had to get all the horses to move. We were inside the house shaking. I told the removalist to take everything he thought would sell and that Id be back to clean up, which of course I wasn't going to do. And so it was that we did a runner and left behind thousands of pounds worth of almost brand new children's toys, feather quilts, cotton bedding, towels, dinner set, pots and pans, carpet and curtains, all things the removalist said he couldn't take. We'd sold our cars, which we'd only had for 3 months, at a huge loss, the day before we left and hired a car to take us to London. For some peculiar reason, for hours on that drive, we were terrified that someone from the Estate Office was following us and would stop us. That's how scared we were. On arrival in London, we gave the Hire Car back and spent a night in a hotel close to the airport.

The following morning we were on a plane back to Australia. Incidentally, a few months later we got an invoice of all the things that had sold at the Auction. We'd made $500, about two hundred pounds. We were devastated. Including air fares, three cars and household effects, the whole disaster had cost us close to a hundred thousand dollars.

While we'd been in the UK, James, who was by then four, had to start school, something we weren't prepared for, as in Australia its Kindy at five then proper school at six. He'd been a troublesome, moody child, but nothing major up till then. He'd only been at school for a week or so when I got a phone call to say he was having to be held down by teachers as he was having a massive meltdown, and could I come to school urgently. They'd tried to call Shelby but couldn't get hold of her. When I arrived at the tiny Primary School, James had FOUR Teachers (There were only five teachers in the school) sitting on him, restraining him. They said he'd gone berserk, throwing furniture etc, swearing the worst profanities you could imagine (I didn't even know he could swear), kicking, biting and punching. I told James to get up off the floor and the teachers to let him go. They were obviously terrified but got up. James then calmly showed me round his class as though nothing happened. From then on it was on. He would have massive outbursts of throwing furniture and toys, swearing and punching. We didn't know what was happening to him. In retrospect, maybe it was just his time to start these attacks, or maybe because of the huge move we'd made from Australia to the UK. He became the devil incarnate when in one of his outbursts and it took its toll on the rest of us. Poor Jade took the brunt. Looking back on it, I think it was already in him but the move across the other side of the world and having to go to 'proper' school could have been the catalyst.(He'd been in full time daycare since three months old so he was used to being away from his family a lot). For whatever reason, poor James's problems would only just have begun.

Arriving back in Australia, we had decided not to go back to Canberra but down to the South Coast town of Batemans Bay, on the east coast. I didn't want to get back on the stressful work bandwagon and we still had enough money to live off for a while, and having lived in Canberra for many years, wanted a change of scenery. After renting a holiday house for a few weeks we soon found a house for Shelby and her two children, and a lovely two story house overlooking the sea for us. Once again we had to buy two lots of absolutely everything, one for Shelby and one for us. We d arrived back with only what could be fitted into suitcases. We had once again sent over some photos and a few other bits from the UK but had to buy two more cars and sets of household goods, as Shelby never had any money. We were very attached to her two children, having had much to do with them both since their birth. Shelby was still not getting any better and continued to go into the Psychiatric Hospital often. Naturally we had the children every time she went in. They were really problematic while they were with her, constantly fighting and arguing, often physically. Shelby could not deal with them and it fell to Ian and I to provide much respite for her, even when out of hospital. When we had them, it would take us a few days to calm them down and get them to stop fighting but as soon as they went back to Shelby it would all start again. My nerves were shattered. I wasn't young anymore and had brought up four children of my own and found it very challenging and stressful having Jade and James. However, we soon found a routine, which was to last us for six years. There was a Country Club, Catalina, where Ian played golf most weekdays and Shelby and I played Bingo while the children were at school. Looking back on it now I don't know how I did it as I now find Bingo mind numbingly boring. James was proving to be very much a problem at school and we had to be called up numerous times by his School to bring him home. His problems seemed to escalate rather than settle down with the new routine and Shelby tried to find a diagnosis for him, without success. Soon we ran out of money and had to apply to Centrelink (our Social Security) and we were put on pensions.

At the ages of seven and eight, the children had become unmanageable for Shelby and our Social Services put them in our care. We had to go to Court three times for this to become legal but I, at least was happy to do it as Id almost had the children from birth regularly. Ian may have wished for a different outcome but supported me nonetheless. The children came to live with us. Luckily we had rented a three bedroom house so they had a bedroom each. During the week, they went to school. James was very problematic and we were often called up to come and pick him up as he'd become unmanageable. Jade, as usual, took the brunt of James' behavior at home and our stress levels were off the scale. James's tantrums had more become violent and we had quite a few incidents where we had to call the police. The Police, however, did nothing to deter him, as he was really cute at that age and the police, once they'd taken him to the Station, would show him round and let him see the cells and try on the police vests. He loved it. He wanted to always be 18, even when he was only 8. We soldiered on with him, and with Jade, who was also traumatised but not to the same level as James. She wouldn't sleep with the light off at night, even to this day, and she's now 14!! It was one of the most stressful times of my life and, although I wouldn't know it then, it was to become worse. The slightest thing would set James off and as time went on and he got older, full blown arguments and almost demonic behavior and tantrums were the norm. His relationship with Jade was the worst. They couldn't be in the same room as each other for most of the time. Finding something to do with the kids at weekends and in the school holidays in Batemans Bay was difficult so we would often make the 4 hour round trip up the Clyde Mountain to Canberra to see my boys and our other grandchildren, plus there was plenty to do in Canberra, Museums and Play Centers. After 5 years in Batemans Bay we decided to move back to Canberra instead of making the regular tedious journeys. And so we moved again, but this time taking a large Removal van with us. At least this time we had all our lovely new furniture with us and not just three suitcases!!

CHAPTER 23

A year before we moved back to Canberra, I asked Shelby if she ever wondered if John, the kids father, who had only seen them at birth, ever thought about them. She'd answered yes, she thought he did do. I asked her if I could ring him and see how he felt about meeting up and seeing them again. When she agreed, I immediately rang him. After the initial shock of hearing from me, he agreed to meet us at a Children's Indoor Play Area in Canberra the following weekend. On the day, we travelled down and sat in the Play Centre waiting for him to arrive. We could see the entry door so knew the moment he walked in. Both kids ran to him, arms outstretched, saying "Daddy!!!!". He put his arms around them and we spent the next two hours really happy. After that, we would see him about once every few months. He lives still with his elderly parents and has recently undergone brain cancer. He is in remission but still is not a well man. He doesn't keep in touch hardly at all with the children but when he does see them he tells them he loves them. So basically they have grown up without a father. He has never offered to give Ian and I a break and take them out for the day, nor offered any money for their support. Its all been down to Ian and I.

Before we moved away from Batemans Bay, we found out that we had to stay in New South Wales in order to receive the money from Social Services for having the children. As this was quite a good amount, we couldn't have done without it. Canberra didn't pay the Allowance so living back there was out of the question. We managed to find a lovely house in a newer suburb 5 minutes from Canberra but still in New South Wales called Jerrabomberra. We bought all new furniture and a puppy, a poodle called Hamish. We thought the change might be good for James. We enrolled him in a large Catholic School that took only boys from ages 9 to 18. They seemed to have a good Support Team and I was honest and upfront about him to them. However, not long after he went there we started getting phone calls asking us to come and get him. He also started to make friends with the Year 10 boys and learnt how to download porn. He continuously kept asking me why he couldn't watch MA Movies, why couldn't he go out on his own. He was 10 at the time. His behavior became such that we had to hide all the knives and scissors in the house as we were becoming scared of him, even at ten years of age. For the year that we spent at that Jerrabomberra house, Jade slept on a mattress on the floor beside our bed, as we couldn't trust James not to do anything to her. Mentally, we could take no more. Physically, I was continually shaking and couldn't stop. We were 61 and should have been enjoying getting ready for retirement.

Along the way we had been taken under the wing of a lovely woman, Cassandra, who worked for an Agency, which dealt with people having trouble with their family dynamics. She was a wonderful support and ear to listen. One day, we were shopping in the Mall and James wanted four large Sushi Rolls. I refused and he became really aggressive. I walked away and we all got in the car. I sat in the back with James, as I couldn't trust him with Jade, and he immediately pulled out a pair of scissors from I don't know where and got a paper bag which was in the back seat pocket and started cutting it up, very slowly and deliberately, getting closer and closer to me and giving me the evil eye. I ignored him all the way home. Once home I told Ian to take Jade out and James and I were left alone. In the kitchen he got himself a drink from the fridge and I took the opportunity to grab the scissors. About five minutes later he came up to me with a metal maths protractor and put the pointed end of it to my throat and said "I know exactly where to stab you with this to kill you." I spent the rest of the day staying out of his way.

The following morning, Cassandra rang me to see how I was going and I told her of this incident. She immediately told Ian and I to go into her office. Once there she looked at the state the pair of us were in, grey faces, shoulders hunched over, and said in a clear voice "That's it. James is not coming home anymore!!" I felt a huge weight lift from my shoulders as Im sure Ian did as well. Cassandra then made some phone calls and got James a place in a Respite Care Home for a fortnight and told us that if DOCS (Our Social Services) hadn't found him somewhere by then there was a place down at the Coast for troubled children where he could go. I felt the relief immediately. Somebody had taken the decision that we should have taken ages ago, but couldn't. It became clear that not his mother, nor Ian or I, could care for James. We got no support whatsoever from our other three boys. Two of them had families of their own and didn't speak to Shelby, so Ian and I taking on her two children, one of whom caused us so much stress, must have made them immune to our suffering. James was collected from school that afternoon by Cassandra and taken straight away to the Respite Home where he stayed for a fortnight. He rang me one day shortly after and asked me if it had been my decision for him not to live with us anymore and I had to say yes. During this fortnight. Cassandra came with us to DOCS to tell them that we could no longer care for James. We were told scornfully that we had to keep caring for him, as they had nobody to take him. We spent an hour in this pathetic man's office being told over and over again that they couldn't take James. In despair, I finally said to him "Tell me, exactly what would it take to have James put in your care?" He said that we would have to get a Lawyer and take DOCS to Court and that it would probably cost us $30,000.

Cassandra said, "Well that's what we'll do". God love her, as soon as we left the office she made an appointment with a local lawyer and we saw him that week. It was a Thursday. By the following Tuesday we were in Court, and James was made a Ward of the State, with DOCS being told off for making us take the case to Court. And so it became just Ian, Jade and me. But my doctor told me I had Post Traumatic Stress Disorder and I've never really recovered. Because we'd lost James' Social Security money, we had to move house as we could no longer afford the high rent we'd been paying in Jerrabomberra, but the overall relief and effect on Ian, Jade and I was enormous. After looking at affordable houses in the area, without success, we decided to move to the other side of Canberra, to a small country town called Yass. It was still in New South Wales so we were still able to get Jade's care money. We found a lovely brand new house in a complex of ten. Jade, who had slept on a mattress on our bedroom floor for a year was able to sleep in a bedroom of her own again. We could leave knives and scissors out. Slowly the main stress disappeared but I still have it to this day and I think I will always be affected by a little boy who could be so beautiful and loving but the devil at other times.

CHAPTER 24

Life for the next 3 years was much easier. Wed had to move house again after we gave our James up as without his money from Social Services, we couldn't afford the huge rent on the house wed been living in, just outside Canberra. We moved to Yass on the opposite side to Canberra, about a 45-minute drive away. James, having spent the two weeks in the Respite Home, had been moved to another Respite Centre down on the South Coast. He would remain here for three months, not going to school and being taken out on excursions and to cafes most days. It was not a normal life for a boy of ten to be living. In December he was moved permanently back to Canberra and started school. We saw him once a fortnight and still do to this day, where he is lovely to us and no problem at all, enjoying his time with us. He is still problematic to his Carers , and is a dreadful worry to me as to how his future will pan out. It seems as though he displays two different sides. He is kind and loving to us now but a demon elsewhere. He wants to come back and live with us and that is why he is so lovely whenever we see him. But while there is the other side of him, there is no chance of him ever coming back to live with us. In Yass, we had enrolled Jade into the local Primary School, but within a short time I became frustrated with her coming out every day crying because she was being bullied. So I decided to pull her out of school and Home School her myself. In New South Wales there is Distance Education for children who lived remotely or could not attend their local school for various reasons and Jade fitted into this system. However it was to take four months before we could start it, so for that time while we waited, I devised a schooling program myself. We bought teaching books, took her to Galleries, Parliament House, Museums, I told her stories about Aborigines, something I had leant about at my days in University. We drew, painted, and did craft. At the time I was doing Scrapbooking and had bought hundreds of dollars worth of Scrapbooking stuff. Jade and I were able to make up some lovely pages together and put them in Albums. For two of my boys, and for Shelby, we made Albums up and put the pages to music on a CD. Really beautiful memories for the them. All in all it was a lovely time. Soon enough though, Distance Education started and we had to learn how to Home School in a different way. Their advice was to try and keep to the school times where possible but in our house this didn't work. Jade wouldn't start work until well into the morning and would often only do an hours work. We had been working like this for a few months when out of the blue she asked to go back to school, this time to the other Primary school in Yass. We enrolled her and she spent the next few months there. One day I received a call from the Headmaster to say she was being disruptive and was going to be put in a Special Class. This was the first time this had happened and was so out of character for her. My feelings are that, during Home Schooling, she had got so far behind in her school work that she didn't know what she was doing with the work in class, she just couldn't do it, so in her boredom became disruptive. As she was in her final year of Primary School she didn't have to stay in that class long as she would soon move up to High School.

When Jade went to High School, we were amazed that she had yet again been put in the Special Class. All her school life, she had been in Main Stream School. Academically, we were told, she wasn't bad but her oppositional behavior was the reason given. There were only a handful of others in her class, of different ages, and right from the beginning she made friends with a girl a year older than her. The class teacher, however, didn't want Jade to be friends with this girl and went out of her way to keep them apart. The teacher also took great pleasure in ringing me almost daily telling me what Jade had done and hadn't done. When I would say something like "Well I will take Jades phone off her tonight", the teacher would, while still on the phone to me, turn to Jade and say "Ha Ha, Your Nan's taking your phone off you tonight". She turned out to be a very spiteful woman who basically ruined Jades chances of ever finding her way in that school. Once again I decided to pull her out and Homeschool her. Again we had to wait months for Distance Education to come through and we relied on books and Gallery visits to keep us going. However, even when Distance Education started (They send you a Term's worth of work in five subjects and you then send a week's worth of work back to them, by Post, each week), Jade would stay in bed until noon or sometimes a bit later and would get up, have brunch and then do half an hours work.

I knew this was wrong but I was so washed out from all I'd been through over the years that I looked forward to her not getting up until noon. It let Ian and I watch some TV or read a book. We were now in our 60's and educating a teenager was not how we'd envisaged our lives. All the time though, I worried about Jade's education, or lack of it in our case. She'd said for a long time that she wanted to be a Pediatric Nurse and I knew the education she as getting from me was nowhere near enough for her to attain that goal. However, again, one day, out of the blue, she said, "Lets move back to Queanbeyan (just outside Canberra where we'd been before when we had our grandson) so that I can go back to school." So that's what we did. We looked at about half a dozen houses to rent there and finally found the one we re in at the moment. It's a lovely house but with quite a big rent so we only just manage financially.

Jade started High School in Year 8 and settled in immediately. However, after a few weeks, she started saying that there were two girls who were being mean to her. Thus started a month long campaign of her being bullied. I went up to the school almost every day to raised eyes from the staff. We even got the local police involved as one of the girls threatened to 'smash Jades face in' and actually threw an apple in her face. It was a horrible time and once again I thought we'd have to go down the Home Schooling route, but this time Jade said NO. She loved it at school and wanted to stay there. By pure coincidence Jade was on Facebook one evening and one of the bullies stuck up for Jade in a conversation she was having with another girl. Later, I told Jade to go and thank the girl the following day. This she did and the girl told the other bully to leave Jade alone and we've had no problems since. It's so good to finally see Jade back at school and happy. She goes into Year 9 after Christmas 2016, and while she has the odd teenage meltdown, is a really lovely girl to have around. She's gone from my baby to my best friend. The only things we don't have in common is clothes and music!!!!!

Since I was a child, I have had Tourette's Syndrome. No, I don't swear but I do, or did till I found the right medication, have numerous tics, or involuntary movements. When I was about eight, I started screwing my eyes up and making little coughing sounds. Although my mum and teachers told me to stop, Tourette's was not known about in Birkenhead, if anywhere, but I was powerless to stop. As I grew older, I developed bad tics in mostly my left side face, abdomen and leg. I was told it was anxiety. I found the condition to be really stressful and tiring, continually moving, or twitching, your muscles. Then, in 1980, aged almost 30, I was sent to a Neurologist in Canberra who immediately diagnosed me, finally, with Tourette's Syndrome. However, now that I had an answer to why I was twitching all the time, I didn't find a cure. I was put on different medications after different medications. Nothing worked. For years I tried everything. Then, in 2004, I was put on a new medication, Risperidone. At last I found something that really reduced the tics. I still had a few small ones but generally they disappeared. I stayed on Risperidone for 11 years. All my life I had been overweight – around the 115 – 120 kilo mark. Id only ever managed to lose weight twice in my 63 years: once when Ian joined the Royal Australian Air Force, and once in England when we'd moved to Dorset and I was writing. These two weight losses were very short lived and I soon found myself back at my usual big weight. I hated being big. I hated getting dressed in the mornings, hated meeting people, going on holiday, everything. Then, in 2014, my youngest sister Diane, also overweight, had a Gastric Bypass and lost 80 kilos. The following year I had severe reflux, so bad that my Specialist said it could kill me. I needed a Fundalipication, a surgical procedure that tightens the opening to the stomach. Only problem was that the Specialist wouldn't do the procedure unless I was under 100 kilos. I tried for 6 months to lose the weight but couldn't. So I decided that I too would have the Gastric Bypass Surgery. I had Private Health Insurance so the surgery would only cost me five thousand dollars. I was told by the Bariatric Surgeon in Canberra that I would have to go to Sydney for the surgery, so this was arranged for late July 2015. However, I'd read that the drug I was on to stop my tics, Risperidone, put, and kept, weight on you, so I decided to stop the medication before my surgery as I wanted to make sure my weight loss surgery had every chance of succeeding. I stopped with my Doctor's advice just a week before my surgery. When I went into hospital, I saw my anaesthetist beforehand and he asked me if I was chewing gum. I wasn't. I was actually sucking my teeth, lips and cheeks. I hadn't noticed I was doing it but he did. For the next 6-8 months my main focus was on losing weight after the surgery. A Gastric Bypass is where the surgeon removes all of your stomach and makes a small pouch for your food and joins it to the small bowel. You can eat very little and, in my case, can't really tolerate sweet things without feeling sick afterwards. But it's a small price to pay for the rewards, if you want them badly enough. I've lost 40 kilos and am now a size 14, where I'd been a 22-24. My Bypass has been a success.   But earlier in 2016, after losing the weight, my mouth sucking came to the forefront of my mind and it became so distressing that I was sent to see a Canberra Neurologist. Over the course of about 4 months, he tried me on 4 different medications. I think he thought it was my Tourette's Syndrome, even though I'd been put on Clonazepam after I'd come off the Risperidone to control my tics. In the end, I was told by the Neurologist that there was nothing else he could offer me, as nothing had worked. In desperation, I rang the Tourette's Association of Australia and asked if they had a Specialist who they could recommend. They did have and a few weeks later I had a Skype Call with him. He is a Neuro Psychiatrist in a large hospital in Sydney. As soon as I told him my story and that I'd come of Risperidone and developed the mouth sucking a few days later, he immediately recognized that I had something called Tardive Dyskonesia. Although this is mainly an untreatable condition, he recommended three medications to try, one after the other if the previous one hadn't worked. Now, I'm on the last one, and its not working. So it looks like I will have to put up with this debilitating problem all my life, unless it mysteriously disappears. It is very distressing and takes up every second of my waking life. Apparently I should have been told by my GP at the time to come off the Risperidone over a period of many months. I should also have been told that I may get Tardive Dyskinesia if I came of it. But I wasn't. I've spoken to a Lawyer who tells me I have a good case to claim compensation so we'll see. But no amount of money could ever compensate for this awful condition.

CHAPTER 25

On my Facebook Page, I have a lovely Group called 'Birkenhead Memories, and, always having liked to write, I started to Post a number of childhood memories from my time living in Birkenhead. I had such a great response to these Posts that people started to say "Why don't you write a book"? So that's what I did. I started this book really, as a Memoir for my children and Grandchildren but I'm hoping there is a wider audience out there for it. By writing down the history of my life, I'm hoping to keep the memories going on well into the future. Too many of us know nothing of our forefather's lives so I'm hoping you will enjoy my journey through life. It has been interesting and stressful, both in equal measures. Having had to raise basically two lots of children, I find that I am worn out, and not having the experiences a normal 64 year old should have. My 3 boys all have successful jobs, Shelby is on new medication which has kept her out of hospital for most of

2016 and all of my other grandchildren are growing up, and they will all achieve what they want to out of life hopefully. And Ian and I, well, we just plod on. He does so much for me and really looks after me and for that I will be eternally grateful to him. So that's where I am today. Having come so far and gone through so much I feel lucky that I'm still alive. I 've got plenty of ideas for a novel and will start writing that soon, but for now, here are my memories. It is impossible to think that in six years' time the two sixteen year olds who eloped to Scotland, went on to have four children and emigrated to Australia, will be seventy. In my head I'm still thirty!!

Writing memories on a Facebook site, I received so many people telling me to write this book. So here it is. I hope you've enjoyed it as much as I've enjoyed writing it. I'm still A Girl From Birkenhead, and always will be.

ABOUT THE AUTHOR

Trish Ollman has been married to Ian since she was 16, and had 2 children by aged 17. She spent the first 21 years of her life in Birkenhead, Merseyside, UK and emigrated to Australia when she was 21 and had 2 more children. In this very entertaining Autobiography of Trish's life, both in the UK and Australia, Trish recounts childhood memories of growing up in a large, poor family, in Birkenhead, as well as her life in Australia with her four children. Trish and Ian now live in Canberra, Australia.

This book recounts a life of innocence and one of bygone days, which Trish hopes will keep the memories alive.

Printed in Great Britain
by Amazon